To: mom

From: Julie

Happy Mother's Day 2001

I love you very much.

# Joy FOR THE JOURNEY

Kathy Babbitt     Joni Eareckson Tada

## Elisabeth Elliot

Claire Cloninger     Liz Curtis Higgs

## Gloria Gaither

Verdell Davis     Jan Carlberg

## Barbara Johnson

Mary Hampton     Susan Alexander Yates

## Gail MacDonald

Laura Lewis Lanier     Barbara Jenkins

## Edith Schaeffer

Anne Ortlund     Elizabeth Skoglund

## Luci Swindoll

Mary Whelchel

J. Countryman is a registered trademark.

A J. Countryman Book

Designed by Koechel Peterson Design, Inc.
Minneapolis, Minnesota

Compiled and Edited by Terri Gibbs

ISBN: 0-8499-5297-2

Printed and bound in Belgium

# JOY

## FOR THE

# JOURNEY

## A WOMAN'S BOOK OF
## JOYFUL PROMISES

# CONTENTS

# THE
# *Joy*
# OF LIFE'S
# LITTLE MOMENTS

There is so much beauty around us,
if we will only take the time to notice it.

Now it happened as they went that He entered a certain village; and a certain woman named Martha welcomed Him into her house. And she had a sister called Mary, who also sat at Jesus' feet and heard His word. But Martha was distracted with much serving, and she approached Him and said, "Lord, do You not care that my sister has left me to serve alone? Therefore tell her to help me." And Jesus answered and said to her, "Martha, Martha, you are worried and troubled about many things. But one thing is needed, and Mary has chosen that good part, which will not be taken away from her."

Luke 10:38–42

# Part One:
# THE JOY OF LIFE'S
# LITTLE MOMENTS

 would like to believe that I have a heart like Mary's, one that stops to listen to God whenever the opportunity arises. I am afraid though, that I probably come much closer to being like Martha. Hurrying about, planning, preparing, fixing, organizing, making lists, and worrying. *Will it all get done?* "It" can be my grocery shopping, the laundry, the meal for the potluck supper later on, the Bible study lesson, my latest craft project, etc., etc., etc.

These thoughts can overtake me during church, while having my devotions, in the midst of prayer—almost anywhere, the still, small voice of the Lord can get drowned out by the shouts of living in the sunset of the twentieth century.

I still believe that the planning, preparing, fixing, and organizing is important. I believe it is important to God. After all, I am trying to be faithful to do well the tasks He has set before me. I need to remember, though, that by far the most important thing I can do is to take the time to sit at Jesus' feet and really *listen.*

Mary Hampton
*Tea and Inspiration*

# PROMISES TO HELP YOU SAVOR EACH MOMENT

Do not worry about tomorrow, for tomorrow will worry about its own things. Sufficient for the day is its own trouble.

🔲 Matthew 6:34

We do not lose heart. Even though our outward man is perishing, yet the inward man is being renewed day by day. For our light affliction, which is but for a moment, is working for us a far more exceeding and eternal weight of glory, while we do not look at the things which are seen, but at the things which are not seen. For the things which are seen are temporary, but the things which are not seen are eternal.

🔲 2 Corinthians 4:16–18

Oh taste and see that the LORD is good;
Blessed is the man who trusts in Him!
Oh, fear the LORD, you His saints!
There is no want to those who fear Him.
The young lions lack and suffer hunger;
But those who seek the LORD shall not
    lack any good thing.

🔲 Psalm 34:8–10

# Savoring each Moment

o experience happiness we must train ourselves to live in this moment, to savor it for what it is, not running ahead in anticipation of some future date nor lagging behind in the paralysis of the past. With wholeness and sensitivity we must live in the here and now. "But what if I don't like the here and now?" you ask. "What if my present moment is one of disappointment or impairment or heartache? How then do I savor that moment?" Good questions. And the answers reside in the first and most profound principle for the art of savoring life: *Pleasure* lies in the heart, not in the happenstance. Our circumstances may be dreadful and riddled with reasons for discouragement or sorrow, but that doesn't mean those moments are utterly devoid of happiness. . . . Those special savored moments of fun, reflection, happiness, and pleasure give us a tiny taste of what eternity with Christ will one day be like.

Luci Swindoll
*You Bring the Confetti*

# PROMISES TO HELP
# YOU RECAPTURE JOY

When wisdom enters your heart,
   And knowledge is pleasant to your soul,
Discretion will preserve you;
Understanding will keep you,
To deliver you from the way of evil. . . .

                                    Proverbs 2:10–11

Blessed are the meek,
   For they shall inherit the earth.
Blessed are those who hunger and thirst
      for righteousness,
For they shall be filled.
Blessed are the merciful,
For they shall obtain mercy.

                                    Matthew 5:5–7

Therefore be imitators of God as dear
children. And walk in love. . . .

                                    Ephesians 5:1–2

# RECAPTURING JOY

s celebrating really that important anyway?

Yes, it is!

Life today is difficult. Problems challenge us and we worry about our children's futures. It's easy to fall into the trap of taking ourselves too seriously, of worrying about success, jobs, acceptance, parenting, illnesses, and so on. It's easy to lose our ability to laugh. It's easy to forget the simple ways of purely enjoying one another. Celebration keeps us balanced in a difficult world, renews our perspective, and enables us to recapture joy. It provides us with an easy means of building friendships within the family. A real benefit of celebration is that it can be very simple and yet the dividends are so great.

Susan Yates
*A House Full of Friends*

# PROMISES TO HELP YOU LOOK FOR BEAUTY

He has made everything beautiful in its time. Also He has put eternity in their hearts, except that no one can find out the work that God does from beginning to end. I know that nothing is better for them than to rejoice and to do good in their lives.

Ecclesiastes 3:11–12

One thing I have desired of the LORD,
That will I seek:
That I may dwell in the house of the LORD
All the days of my life,
To behold the beauty of the LORD,
And to inquire in His temple.

Psalm 27:4

Give unto the LORD the glory due to
His name;
Worship the LORD in the beauty
of holiness.

Psalm 29:2

# LOOKING FOR BEAUTY

here is so much beauty around us, if we will only take the time to notice it. You can make a conscious effort to look for the essence and therefore develop an appreciation for the beautiful things in life. Your days will seem a lot less harried, I promise you. Beauty has a way of totally capturing our senses, making us forget the fact that the car stalled on the way to work this morning, that the kids spilled chocolate milk on the carpet, that the workload keeps piling up. For a few brief shining moments, nothing else seems to matter. And the wonderful thing about beauty is that we can store it in our minds to be played over and over again.

Luci Swindoll
*You Bring the Confetti*

# PROMISES THAT ENCOURAGE YOU TO CELEBRATE VICTORIES

I will praise You, O LORD, with my whole heart;
I will tell of all Your marvelous works.
I will be glad and rejoice in You;
I will sing praise to Your name, O Most High.

Psalm 9:1–2

Behold, this is our God;
We have waited for Him, and He will save us.
This is the LORD;
We have waited for Him;
We will be glad and rejoice in His salvation.

Isaiah 25:9

I will sing of the mercies of the LORD forever;
With my mouth will I make known Your
faithfulness to all generations.

Psalm 89:1

# CELEBRATING VICTORIES

t is important in our lives and work that we celebrate our little victories as they come. If we wait for something major to celebrate, we will miss much of the potential joy in our lives. I believe it is the overworked, under-rewarded men and women who reach midlife and look up one day to ask, "Is that all there is?"

A songwriter's work is completed long before the release of the album. By the time the record and printed product are released, I am deeply involved in another project, and the edge is off the celebration mood. So I have learned not to wait to celebrate the completion of my work. When a musical is recorded and I have a rough mix of the album in my hands, I rush home to Mobile, ready to gather a few good friends for a celebration. That is when I'm weary from the work, excited about the results, and elated by a sense of accomplishment. I have learned that is the time to celebrate.

Claire Cloninger
*When God Shines Through*

# PROMISES TO HELP YOU FIND FULFILLMENT

My soul shall be satisfied as with
marrow and fatness,
And my mouth shall praise You with
joyful lips.

🔖 Psalm 63:5

Delight yourself also in the LORD,
And He shall give you the desires of your heart.

🔖 Psalm 37:4

As for me, I will see Your face in righteousness;
I shall be satisfied when I awake in Your
likeness.

🔖 Psalm 17:15

# FINDING FULFILLMENT

 re you in a rut? Do you feel trapped by your circumstances? Would you like to break out and do something totally new and different? Every woman feels confined at one time or another in her life. She may feel stagnant in her job, tied down to young children, locked in a bad marriage, or obligated as the caretaker of a chronically ill relative. There are many difficult circumstances that cause women to be unable to live a carefree life, and you may be in the midst of one. . . .

As a woman of adventure, I have lived a life of extremes and know the exhilaration and pain of tent camping alongside the road in all kinds of weather to living in a nice, warm, and comfortable suburban home. And I have learned that a life of adventure is not limited by circumstances or money. Women of adventure have conquered their fates and know how to live exciting and fulfilling lives right where they are. They have learned to reinvent themselves and find creative ways to enjoy the world and their place in it. They know how to take mini-vacations, stop and smell the roses, and live fully in the moment.

Barbara Jenkins
*Wit and Wisdom for Women*

# PROMISES TO HELP YOU FIND JOY IN YOUR WORK

In all the work you are doing, work the best you can. Work as if you were doing it for the Lord, not for people.

Colossians 3:23

I can do all things through Christ, because he gives me strength.

Philippians 4:13

*Those who work hard make a profit, but those who only talk will be poor.*

Proverbs 14:23

The LORD gives strength to his people; the LORD blesses his people with peace.

Psalm 29:11

# FINDING JOY IN YOUR WORK

ork should always be associated with joy. . . .

The story is told of three women washing clothes. A passerby asked each what she was doing.

"Washing clothes" was the first answer.

"A bit of household drudgery" was the second.

"I'm mothering three young children who someday will fill important and useful spheres in life, and wash-day is a part of my grand task in caring for these souls who shall live forever" was the third.

Ordinary work, which is what most of us do most of the time, is ordained by God every bit as much as is the extraordinary. All work done for God is spiritual work and therefore not merely a duty but a holy privilege.

Elisabeth Elliot
*The Shaping of a Christian Family*

# PROMISES TO HELP
# YOU FIND HOLINESS IN
# THE ORDINARY

Blessed be the LORD,
Who daily loads us with benefits,
The God of our salvation!

Psalm 68:19

My little children, let us not love in word
or in tongue, but in deed and in truth. And
by this we know that we are of the truth,
and shall assure our hearts before Him.

1 John 3:18

*The light of the eyes rejoices the heart,*
*And a good report makes the bones healthy.*

Proverbs 15:30

In the morning sow your seed,
And in the evening do not withhold
your hand;
For you do not know which will prosper,
Either this or that,
Or whether both alike will be good.

Ecclesiastes 11:6

# FINDING HOLINESS IN THE ORDINARY

enri Nouwen, in his book *Out of Solitude*, tells of an old Notre Dame professor who had always complained that his work was constantly being interrupted. Like so many of us, he longed for the freedom to concentrate fully on what he considered important. Late in his life, however, the professor came to realize what he wished he had known all along: that *the interruptions were his work. . . .*

The interruptions *are* the work. The pieces *are* the whole. We cannot wait for a total, personal revelation of all that God has for us to be handed down in one lump sum. God reveals Himself to us bit by spiritual bit. Even our broadest visions and our highest goals, once we know them, must be broken down and lived out in the small particulars of our everyday lives if they are to have meaning.

Claire Cloninger
*When God Shines Through*

# PROMISES TO HELP YOU UNDERSTAND YOUR EMOTIONS

Serve the LORD with gladness;
Come before His presence with singing.
Know that the LORD, He is God;
It is He who has made us, and not we
    ourselves;
We are His people and the sheep of
    His pasture.

Psalm 100:2–3

Hear my prayer, O LORD,
And let my cry come to You.
Do not hide Your face from me in the day
    of my trouble;
Incline Your ear to me;
In the day that I call, answer me speedily.

Psalm 102:2

Humble yourselves under the mighty hand
of God, that He may exalt you in due time,
casting all your care upon Him, for He cares
for you.

1 Peter 5:6–7

# Understanding Your Emotions

he difference in estrogen levels in a woman's body during various times of the month correlates to a predictable pattern of behaviors and emotions. In general, during the first week of her cycle she is outgoing, ambitious, optimistic . . . and self-confident. During the second week she is hopeful, easygoing, creative, . . . and has inner strength and a sense of well-being. . . .

The third week she lacks coordination, longs for peace, . . . is impatient, . . . and gloomy. The fourth week she is very irritable, touchy, withdrawn, . . . and lacks self-confidence.

Whew! Is it any wonder that interpersonal conflicts sometimes seem to come from nowhere? Naturally, these characteristics are not true for all women, and some women struggle with them more than others (and their families struggle right along with them).

Maybe you need to tell yourself, "Tomorrow or next week will be better" or "It will soon pass, just hang in there!"

Kathy Babbitt
*Habits of the Heart*

# PROMISES TO HELP YOU ACCEPT YOUR BODY CYCLES

To everything there is a season,
A time for every purpose under heaven . . .
A time to plant,
And a time to pluck what is planted . . .
A time to break down,
And a time to build up;
A time to weep,
And a time to laugh.

Ecclesiastes 3:1–4

I will praise You, for I am fearfully and
    wonderfully made,
Marvelous are Your works,
And that my soul knows very well.
My frame was not hidden from You,
When I was made in secret,
And skillfully wrought in the lowest parts
    of the earth.

Psalm 139:14–15

# ACCEPTING YOUR
# BODY CYCLES

omen are always aware of their
bodies. Changes within our
hormonal balances are always
sending us signals that can affect
moods, strength levels, and even our perceptual
capacities. If we don't understand those things,
thinking positively about them and accepting
them, our bodies can betray us and leave us in
a nongrowth predicament.

A fellow-learner in a class I taught shared
thoughts about the tendency of many women
to fight depression in the fall of the year. She
reminded us that Psalm 1 suggests that we are all
to be like trees planted by a stream—trees which
bear fruit "in . . . season."

Her insight? That even trees don't flower and
bear fruit all the time—only in season. But men
and women alike seem to think that we should
be bearing fruit all the time; we punish ourselves
when we're not. She was teaching us the beauty
of personal dormancy: We must allow for it and
accept it joyfully. . . . A time of inner strength-
gathering for a better bloom later.

Gail MacDonald
*High Call, High Privilege*

# THE
# *Joy*
## OF FRIENDSHIP

*A friend is someone who accepts you—
warts, wrinkles, weight, and all—unconditionally.*

Now it happened one day that Elisha went to
Shunem, where there was a notable woman,
and she persuaded him to eat some food. So
it was, as often as he passed by, he would turn
in there to eat some food. And she said to her
husband, "Look now, I know that this is a holy
man of God, who passes by us regularly. Please,
let us make a small upper room on the wall;
and let us put a bed for him there, and a table
and a chair and a lampstand; so it will be,
whenever he comes to us, he can turn in there."

2 Kings 4:8–10

# PART TWO:
## THE JOY OF FRIENDSHIP

ome people have the gift of hospitality. This well-to-do woman from Shunem was one of them. She used her means to bless and refresh others. She had discerned that Elisha was God's prophet, but she also knew that he was hungry and tired. She and her husband anticipated his needs for rest, reflection, and reading. They gave the best they had, and God rewarded them by giving this childless couple a son. God rewarded her hospitality to His prophet with the desire of her heart.

When was the last time you were refreshed by the hospitality of one of God's thoughtful children? Refresh someone soon with a body and soul stopover at your expense and for God's pleasure.

Jan Carlberg
*The Hungry Heart*

# PROMISES ABOUT ENJOYING FRIENDSHIP

*A friend loves at all times,*
*And a brother is born for adversity.*

Proverbs 17:17

This is my commandment, that you love one another as I have loved you. Greater love has no one than this, than to lay down one's life for his friends.

John 15:12–13

And if one member suffers, all the members suffer with it; or if one member is honored, all the members rejoice with it.

1 Corinthians 12:26

Let brotherly love continue. Do not forget to entertain strangers, for by so doing some have unwittingly entertained angels.

Hebrews 13:1–2

# ENJOYING FRIENDSHIP

 hen the chips are down, there's nothing like a good girlfriend. A friend is someone who accepts you—warts, wrinkles, weight, and all—unconditionally. She will listen to you cry or complain and do her best to look out for your best interests. . . . She supports you through thick and thin, but because there is mutual respect, she will not allow you to wallow in self-pity or manipulate her. She will encourage you to be your best self and allow you the freedom to make your own choices.

All women are born with the need to communicate at a deeper level with their mothers, grandmothers, sisters, daughters, aunts, cousins, and other significant females in their lives. Wholesome friendships among women promote sound mental and emotional health. Friends remind us we are part of something greater than ourselves, a larger world, and the right friends keep us on track.

Barbara Jenkins
*Wit and Wisdom for Women*

# PROMISES ABOUT NEEDING EACH OTHER

Two are better than one,
Because they have a good reward
 for their labor.
For if they fall, one will lift up his companion.
But woe to him who is alone when he falls,
For he has no one to help him up.

Ecclesiastes 4:9

Everyone helped his neighbor,
And said to his brother,
"Be of good courage!"

Isaiah 41:6

Whoever does the will of My Father in heaven
is My brother and sister and mother.

Matthew 12:50

For as the body is one and has many
members, but all the members of that one
body, being many are one body, so also is
Christ. For by one Spirit we were all baptized
into one body.

1 Corinthians 12:12

# NEEDING EACH OTHER

e cannot grow alone. We are all interconnected, and we need one another. We grow only as each part does its work.

Jesus Himself needed the extended family of believers to fill in a gap for Him. As He hung on the cross in agony, knowing His death was close, He looked out into the crowd and saw His beloved mother. His pain in seeing her pain must have been overwhelming. With a broken heart and eyes filled with tears, He gazed tenderly at her. And then He saw the disciple whom He loved standing nearby.

Jesus said to His mother, "Dear woman, here is your son," and to the disciple, "Here is your mother." From that time on, this disciple took her into his home.

John, Jesus' beloved disciple, became a son in Mary's extended family. He filled the gap that Jesus left when He died.

Yes, God created us to live in a family. And it is good.

Susan Yates
*A House Full of Friends*

# PROMISES TO HELP YOU ENJOY GOD'S COLORFUL CREATION

For as we have many members in one body, but all the members do not have the same function, so we, being many, are one body in Christ, and individually members of one another. Having then gifts differing according to the grace that is given to us, let us use them. . . .

🌑 Romans 12:4–6

There are diversities of gifts, but the same Spirit. There are differences of ministries, but the same Lord. And there are diversities of activities, but it is the same God who works all in all.

🌑 1 Corinthians 12:4–6

If there is any consolation in Christ, if any comfort of love, if any fellowship of the Spirit . . . if any affection and mercy, fulfill my joy by being like-minded, having the same love, being of one accord of one mind.

🌑 Philippians 2:1–2

# ENJOYING GOD'S
# COLORFUL CREATION

 see the "color" of God's creation not only in the visual beauty of the world around me. I am also learning to see it in the incredibly diverse beauty of His children as well. Each of us has been made so uniquely, designed so specifically, that there is not one other person on earth exactly like us. We truly are what my friend Mickey Smith calls "human snowflakes." Every finger on every hand on every person in every land who has ever lived contains a unique fingerprint!

What a colorful creation this is! Think of it. God has delighted to give each one of us a special identity, and yet many of us spend our lives trying to conform to some self imposed "norm." We deny our own individuality and that of others. We insist on playing out God's drama in black and white, ignoring the many colorful brushstrokes of His hand.

If there is any place on earth where creativity and individuality should flourish, it should be in the church of Jesus Christ.

Claire Cloninger
*When God Shines Through*

# PROMISES TO HELP YOU ENJOY GIVING TO OTHERS

Give, and it will be given to you: good
measure, pressed down, shaken together,
and running over will be put into your
bosom. For with the same measure that
you use, it will be measured back to you.

> Luke 6:38

She extends her hand to the poor,
Yes, she reaches out her hands to the needy.

> Proverbs 31:20

He who gives to the poor will not lack,
But he who hides his eyes will have
many curses.

> Proverbs 28:27

Defend the poor and fatherless;
Do justice to the afflicted and needy.
Deliver the poor and needy;
Free them from the hand of the wicked.

> Psalm 82:3–4

# GIVING TO OTHERS

ost of us grew up hearing the golden rule: "Do unto others as you would have them do unto you." God pushes His children beyond their personal back yards to a *global* golden rule. Linked by satellites, computers, television, and jet travel, we know of worlds beyond our small one. But with knowledge comes responsibility. Personal, national, and global costs skyrocket when we knowingly do wrong or purposely withhold our help. To obey God's global golden rule is to love as God loves. Giving God's love never harms the giver or the recipient.

You make a world of difference as you obey God's global golden rule.

Jan Carlberg
*The Hungry Heart*

# PROMISES TO HELP
# YOU SERVE OTHERS

A new commandment I give to you, that
you love one another; as I have loved you, that
you also love one another. By this all will know
that you are My disciples, if you have love for
one another.

John 13:34–35

And whoever desires to be first among you,
let him be your slave—just as the Son of Man
did not come to be served, but to serve, and
to give His life a ransom for many.

Matthew 20:27–28

*You, brethren, have been called to
liberty; only do not use liberty as an
opportunity for the flesh, but through
love serve one another.*

Galatians 5:13

# SERVING OTHERS

he blessings that come from reaching out to others cannot be overestimated. I learn this anew every year around Christmas. We usually have several dozen families who have lost a loved one during the year, either from AIDS, suicide, or some other tragedy. So over the years I have started around December 14 . . . and I set aside everything else and start telephoning the families who have experienced a loss.

Usually when I get them on the phone it takes a minute for them to connect ME with the person who writes the books and sends them newsletters. Then they call another person to the phone, and soon every phone in the house has a family member talking. They appreciate that someone cared enough to remember their loss at holiday time. Their reaction proves the truth of that adage:

People don't care how much you know.

They just need to know you CARE.

Barbara Johnson
*I'm So Glad You Told Me*
*What I Didn't Wanna Hear*

# PROMISES ABOUT REACHING BEYOND OURSELVES

By this we know love, because He laid down His life for us. And we also ought to lay down our lives for the brethren. But whoever has this world's goods, and sees his brother in need, and shuts up his heart from him, how does the love of God abide in him?

1 John 3:16–17

And whoever gives one of these little ones only a cup of cold water in the name of a disciple, assuredly, I say to you, he shall by no means lose his reward.

Matthew 10:42

Whoever receives one little child like this in My name receives Me.

Matthew 18:5

# REACHING BEYOND OURSELVES

M y heart's desire is to find more opportunities to give myself away and teach my children the joy of service at the same time. One little problem: *when*?! A friend of mine once moaned, "There's just not enough of *me* to go around." Lots of us feel the same way and can't bear the thought of adding one more activity, one more to do item to our list, however worthy it may be.

For busy women like us, who don't know how we could manage the added role of volunteer, psychologist Virginia O'Leary offers a word of encouragement: "The more roles women have, the better off they are, and the less likely they are to be depressed or discouraged about their lives. When we have a lot to do, we complain that it's driving us crazy—but, in fact, it's what keeps us sane."

It's ironic that one of the best remedies for impending burnout is to give yourself away. To pick one time and place each week where you stretch out your hands for the pure joy of doing it.

Liz Curtis Higgs
*Only Angels Can Wing It*

# PROMISES TO HELP YOU LIFT OTHERS UP

Rejoice with those who rejoice, and weep
with those who weep. Be of the same mind
toward one another. Do not set your mind
on high things, but associate with the humble.
Do not be wise in your own opinion.

Romans 12:15–16

Therefore comfort each other and edify
one another, just as you also are doing.

1 Thessalonians 5:11

Let us pursue the things which make for peace
and the things by which one may edify another.

Romans 14:19

# LIFTING OTHERS UP

 here's something deep within us that loves to be first, to win, to be "in." We elbow up through degrees, titles, possessions, rights, privileges, connections, seniority, and the like. But once we reach our goals, then what? God doesn't separate us from those who are lower on the career ladder than we are. He tells us to pull them up with us. "Love him as yourself, for you were aliens in Egypt. I am the LORD your God" (Leviticus 19:34). In a few words God both levels and lifts us: "You were an alien, too," and "I am your Lord God."

Do you know someone who needs a lift today?

Jan Carlberg
*The Hungry Heart*

# PROMISES TO HELP YOU LEARN FROM OTHERS

*Let him who is taught the word share in all good things with him who teaches.*

Galatians 6:6

*L*ikewise you younger people, submit yourselves to your elders. Yes, all of you be submissive to one another, and be clothed with humility, for God resists the proud, but gives grace to the humble.

1 Peter 5:5

*W*hoever loves instruction loves knowledge, But he who hates correction is stupid.

Proverbs 12:1

# LEARNING FROM OTHERS

o learn, you must want to be taught. . . .

I think it was Mark Twain, Grandma Moses, or someone equally perceptive who said, "Learn from the mistakes of others: you can't live long enough to make all the mistakes yourself." Anyway, that statement is one of the lessons life works hard at teaching us all.

No matter how efficient, smart, or independent we happen to think ourselves to be, sooner or later we run into a "brick wall" that our intelligence or experience cannot handle for us. We can fake it, avoid it, or blunder through it. But a better solution would be to find someone who has walked that way before and has gained wisdom from the experience.

Gloria Gaither
*Decisions*

# PROMISES ABOUT THE JOY OF FELLOWSHIP

And let us consider one another in order to stir up love and good works, not forsaking the assembling of ourselves together, as is the manner of some, but exhorting one another, and so much the more as you see the Day approaching.

Hebrews 10:24–25

But if we walk in the light as He is in the light, we have fellowship with one another, and the blood of Jesus Christ His Son cleanses us from all sin.

1 John 1:7

# ENJOYING FELLOWSHIP

 poet once described friends as "the sunshine of life." I myself have found that the day is certainly much brighter when I'm sharing it with my friends. Enjoying fellowship is one of life's sweetest blessings and joys. What would we do without people and the many shadings of companionship and camaraderie? We need friends in our lives, friends with whom we not only discuss "deep" issues and confide our secrets, fears, or sorrows, but with whom we can laugh, play, and even cry. The best times in life are made a thousand times better when shared with a dear friend.

Camaraderie is definitely a part of friendship, and camaraderie itself can often produce friendships, too. When we reach out to others, they reach out to us. It's a two-way street, a street practically lined with balloons and streamers in celebration of the unique bonds of friendship.

Luci Swindoll
*You Bring the Confetti*

THE
Joy
OF WALKING
WITH CHRIST

*Let every part of your life—your person, your style,
your direction, your flavor—be in Him.*

$\mathcal{A}$ certain woman of the wives of the sons of the prophets cried out to Elisha, saying, "Your servant my husband is dead, and you know that your servant feared the LORD. And the creditor is coming to take my two sons to be his slaves."

So Elisha said to her, "What shall I do for you? Tell me, what do you have in the house?" And she said, "Your maidservant has nothing in the house but a jar of oil."

Then he said, "Go, borrow vessels from everywhere. . . . And when you have come in, you shall shut the door behind you and your sons; then pour it into all those vessels, and set aside the full ones."

So she went from him and shut the door behind her and her sons, who brought the vessels to her; and she poured it out. Now it came to pass, when the vessels were full, . . . the oil ceased. Then she came and told the man of God. And he said, "Go, sell the oil and pay your debt; and you and your sons live on the rest."

2 Kings 4:1–7

# PART THREE: THE JOY OF WALKING WITH CHRIST

 ow many times in different ways has the Lord said simply, "Yield up the pieces, the scraps, the leftovers of your lives. All you've got is all I need to make a mountain from your molehill of faith"?

He said that through Elisha to a woman who came to the prophet in great distress. Her sons were about to be sold into slavery as a settlement for her late husband's debts.

"What have we to work with?" Elisha asked. The widow had one small container of oil—nothing else of value.

"Gather up all of your empty vessels—whatever old pots and pitchers you can find or borrow," the prophet commended, "and begin to fill them with oil."

The widow did as she was bid, and she found to her amazement that there was enough oil to fill every vessel—enough to pay the debt and keep her family for life. . . .

Whatever your life's circumstances may be, these are the very things we are to yield to our Lord. He stands ready to transform all that we offer (when it is all that we have) into all that we need.

Claire Cloninger
*When God Shines Through*

# PROMISES ABOUT SEEKING GOD

O God, You are my God;
Early will I seek You;
My soul thirsts for You;
My flesh longs for You
In a dry and thirsty land
Where there is no water.

Psalm 63:1

Seek the LORD and His strength;
Seek His face evermore!
Remember His marvelous works which
 He has done,
His wonders, and the judgments of His mouth.

1 Chronicles 16:11–12

If you confess with your mouth the Lord
Jesus and believe in your heart that God has
raised Him from the dead, you will be saved.

Romans 10:9

# SEEKING GOD

ost children love to play hide and seek. No one wants to be found immediately, but neither do they want to remain hidden and forgotten. God promises to be visible to all wholehearted seekers. God doesn't play games with us, even seemingly harmless ones like hide and seek. And for all who find Him, it's an eternal case of finder's keepers.

Are you trying to play games with God? God places Himself in the open for all wholehearted seekers and presents His much-sought-after children with everlasting love and long-range plans.

Jan Carlberg
*The Hungry Heart*

# PROMISES ABOUT GOD'S FORGIVENESS

There is therefore now no condemnation to those who are in Christ Jesus, who do not walk according to the flesh, but according to the Spirit. For the law of the Spirit of life in Christ Jesus has made me free from the law of sin and death.

Romans 8:1–2

If we confess our sins, He is faithful and just to forgive us our sins and to cleanse us from all unrighteousness.

1 John 1:9

You have forgiven the iniquity of Your people; You have covered all their sin.

Psalm 85:2

# FORGIVEN BY GOD

ecrets lurk inside most of us like buried treasure, even though their value is dubious. Some people assume their secrets are safe, since they remain convinced that God does not exist. Others are too busy covering their sins to consider the consequences. However we handle our secrets, two truths remain: nothing hides from God, and no one escapes the woe of secret sins. Trust God with your confessions and repentance. The God who sees and knows your secret sins also sees and knows your broken heart. And He forgives.

Jan Carlberg
*The Hungry Heart*

# PROMISES ABOUT BEING RECONCILED TO GOD

Now all things are of God, who has reconciled us to Himself through Jesus Christ, and has given us the ministry of reconciliation, that is, that God was in Christ reconciling the world to Himself.

2 Corinthians 5:18–19

For you did not receive the spirit of bondage again to fear, but you received the Spirit of adoption by whom we cry out, "Abba, Father." The Spirit Himself bears witness with our spirit that we are children of God.

Romans 8:15–16

For it pleased the Father that in Him all the fullness should dwell and by Him to reconcile all things to Himself, by Him, whether things on earth or things in heaven, having made peace through the blood of His cross.

Colossians 1:19–20

# RECONCILED TO GOD

erhaps God's most beautiful gift to the believer is His provision for forgiveness and reconciliation [friendship]. It cost Him everything— the life and death of His Son. It costs us so little by comparison—only that we be willing to confess each wrong thought or deed or attitude and turn back to Him. Yet so often we let sins fester unconfessed beneath the surface of our lives.

One vital ingredient in our relationship with Jesus is our willingness to be honest with Him. He found it easy to be friends with harlots and tax collectors because they were honest with Him about their sinfulness. And He asks the same honesty of us. . . .

Christians whose lives are transparent before the Father see themselves as sinners. They understand grace and praise God for it. Because they know their forgiveness was not bought cheaply, they take it very seriously.

Claire Cloninger
*When God Shines Through*

# PROMISES ABOUT BEING REFINED BY GOD

If anyone cleanses himself from [dishonor], he will be a vessel for honor, sanctified and useful for the Master, prepared for every good work.

2 Timothy 2:21

LORD, you have heard the desire of the humble;
You will prepare their heart;
You will cause Your ear to hear.

Psalm 10:17

It is God who arms me with strength,
And makes my way perfect.

Psalm 18:32

# REFINED BY GOD

 od is love. His will is love. His law is His love. His love is His law. It is a grossly distorted view of God Himself and of His love that finds the idea of His chastening us intolerable. Can we forget that He took our punishment on Himself before the foundation of the world? He was the Lamb slain. He loved us then. He loved us enough to pay the death penalty. Shall He love us less now? Those who come to God come to a Consuming Fire. We easily forget that, looking for an indulgent grandfather whose love, a mere sentiment, capitulates to our whims and overlooks our selfishness. God will not do that, for to do so would be to damn us. He is not willing that any be damned.

The Consuming Fire must do His work burning, purging, refining—for His object is our perfection. How could His love want less than that?

Elisabeth Elliot
*The Shaping of a Christian Family*

# PROMISES TO GIVE US CONFIDENCE IN CHRIST

Being confident of this very thing, that He who has begun a good work in you will complete it until the day of Jesus Christ.

Philippians 1:3

In you, O Lord, I put my trust;
Let me never be put to shame.
Deliver me in Your righteousness,
    and cause me to escape;
Incline Your ear to me, and save me. . . .
For You are my hope, O Lord God
You are my trust from my youth.

Psalm 71:1, 2, 5

It is better to trust in the Lord
Than to put confidence in man.

Psalm 118:8

# CONFIDENT IN CHRIST

e have all known women who were strong, but not very honorable. Our television screens are filled with them. And there are women who are honorable, but frankly, not very strong. The first setback or the first perceived threat, and they fold up like a card table.

The kind of women most of us long to be are both strong and honorable, clothed with the kind of power that comes from on high, certain of our value in God's eyes, definite in our calling, and moving forward with complete assurance. Francis De Sales said, "Nothing is so strong as gentleness, nothing so gentle as real strength."

Liz Curtis Higgs
*Only Angels Can Wing It*

# PROMISES ABOUT BEING GENUINE

*B*ehold what manner of love the Father has bestowed on us, that we should be called children of God! Therefore the world does not know us, because it did not know Him.

🔖 1 John 3:1

*F*or you are all sons of God through faith in Christ Jesus. . . . There is neither Jew nor Greek, there is neither slave nor free, there is neither male nor female; for you are all one in Christ Jesus. And if you are Christ's then you are Abraham's seed, and heirs according to the promise.

🔖 Galatians 3:26, 28, 29

*H*e has shown you, O man, what is good;
And what does the LORD require of you
But to do justly,
To love mercy,
And to walk humbly with your God?

🔖 Micah 6:8

# Genuine in Christ

 e are the most appealing to others, and the happiest within, when we are completely ourselves. But it is a constant struggle because, as Scripture teaches, the world is always trying to press us into its mold. The mold of the world is the mold of the synthetic, the mold of the artificial, the mold of the celluloid—the "Plastic Person."

The world cries, "You've got to be young and you've got to be tan. You've got to be thin and you've got to be rich. You've got to be great." But Scripture says, "You don't have to be any of those things. You simply have to be yourself—at any age—as God made you, available to Him so that He can work in and through you to bring about His kingdom and His glory." Now relax. Trust Him and be yourself!

Luci Swindoll
*You Bring the Confetti*

# PROMISES TO HELP YOU GROW IN CHRIST

That we should no longer be children, tossed to and fro and carried about with every wind of doctrine, by the trickery of men, in the cunning craftiness of deceitful planning, but speaking the truth in love, may grow up in all things unto Him who is the head—Christ.

Ephesians 4:14–15

*But be ye doers of the word, and not hearers only, deceiving yourselves.*

James 1:22

I am the vine, you are the branches. He who abides in Me, and I in him, bears much fruit; for without Me you can do nothing.

John 15:5

# GROWING IN CHRIST

I n order to be a child of God, we have to change; that's what Jesus said. We have to admit we can't get there the way we are and be willing to humble ourselves and change. . . .

Remember that God's love for you is absolutely steadfast, and unlike humans, he does not give or take away his love based on your performance or your qualifications. It will not take God by surprise when you discover an area in your life that is less than what it should be. He knows it already, and even knowing all there is to know about you, his love and concern for you have not budged one inch.

Mary Whelchel
*How to Thrive from 9 to 5*

# PROMISES TO HELP YOU DEVELOP GODLY HABITS

And we have known and believed the love that God has for us. God is love, and he who abides in love abides in God, and God in him.

🔲 1 John 4:16

And a servant of the Lord must not quarrel but be gentle to all, able to teach, patient.

🔲 2 Timothy 2:24

Do not be ashamed of the testimony of our Lord . . . who has saved us and called us with a holy calling, not according to our works, but according to His own purpose and grace which was given to us in Christ Jesus before time began.

🔲 2 Timothy 1:8–9

# DEVELOPING GODLY HABITS

 ome people continuously act on impulse, grabbing at whatever seems attractive at the moment. Now some spontaneity is healthy, but when we face all of life with a senseless striving to satisfy our impulses, we defeat ourselves.

Sometimes we do what we do to escape what we perceive to be more threatening, demanding, or painful. We may put up with a dirty house because it is unpleasant to wash the kitchen floor, or we may avoid working out conflicts because it is painful to face our weaknesses.

We need to make conscious decisions in order to change. Our aim is to develop godly habits that result in godly living.

Kathy Babbitt
*Habits of the Heart*

# PROMISES ABOUT SERVING GOD

*If anyone serves Me, let him follow Me; and where I am, there My servant will be also. If anyone serves Me, him My Father will honor.*

John 12:26

You shall worship the LORD your God, and Him only you shall serve.

Matthew 4:10

And the people said to Joshua, "The LORD our God we will serve, and His voice we will obey!"

Joshua 24:24

# SERVING GOD

 woman makes an enormous leap forward in her spiritual development when she determines that being useful is more important than being *noticed.* I am appalled at how often our culture urges us to place priority attention on our physical appearance. We thus become mindful of the things that are evaluated in terms of size and shape. And listening to this "cultural mandate," we can be tempted to try to become very beautiful—and useless. . . .

If there is a beginning point in spiritual development, it is the choice one makes to become useful to God and, therefore, to others. I have a right to make this choice because I begin with the assumption that having been made by God, I am alive for a purpose.

Gail MacDonald
*High Call, High Privilege*

# PROMISES ABOUT MAKING WISE CHOICES

Then He said to them all, "If anyone desires to come after Me, let him deny himself, and take up his cross daily, and follow Me. For whoever desires to save his life will lose it, but whoever loses his life for My sake will save it."

🔲 Luke 9:23–24

Mary . . . sat at Jesus' feet and heard His word. . . . And Jesus answered and said . . . "Martha, Martha, you are worried and troubled about many things. But one thing is needed, and Mary has chosen that good part, which will not be taken away from her."

🔲 Luke 10:39, 41

Let the words of my mouth and the
    meditation of my heart
Be acceptable in Your sight,
O Lord, my strength and my Redeemer.

🔲 Psalm 19:14

# MAKING WISE CHOICES

S. Lewis once said, "No clever arrangement of bad eggs ever made a good omelette." What we truly are will dictate our choices, no matter how we try to camouflage or hide it, and no amount of moral effort will make us choose rightly if our hearts aren't right. Sooner or later the pressures and pace of our lives will expose what we really are. . . .

Morality would be a cumbersome burden if each decision of our lives had to be carefully checked against some itemized, written code. We would be in constant turmoil worrying about whether some code was overlooked or misinterpreted. The joy of right living would be strangled in legalism. But it is exactly this sort of system that was in effect before Jesus brought the renovation of the human heart and motives through His death and resurrection and then provided us with the live-in support of the Holy Spirit. . . .

Good choices come most freely from the purist possible motives; these come from a heart repossessed by the transforming power of love. Love does what law could never do.

Gloria Gaither
*Decisions*

# PROMISES ABOUT LIVING IN CHRIST

For in Him dwells all the fullness of the godhead bodily; and you are complete in Him, who is the head of all principality and power.

> Colossians 2:9–10

*Not that we are sufficient of ourselves to think of anything as being from ourselves, but our sufficiency is from God.*

> 2 Corinthians 3:4–5

For whatever is born of God overcomes the world. And this is the victory that has overcome the world—our faith. Who is he who overcomes the world, but he who believes that Jesus is the son of God?

> 1 John 5:4–5

# LIVING IN CHRIST

et every part of your life—your person, your style, your direction, your flavor—be in Him. When you're in Him, then you're based on truth. You'll be honest and genuine through and through; you'll be coordinated, all of a piece; you'll be in harmony with yourself. And then you can grow within yourself to unlimited dimensions—and all because you're in God.

Faddish lives age quickly. They're not based on God, who is greater than all culture and all generations, so twenty years from now they'll seem faded and "out of it." Anchor yourself to the great "I AM," and you will develop more and more into a woman who is ageless, whole, true, and at rest.

Anne Ortlund
*Disciplines of the Heart*

# PROMISES TO HELP YOU REFLECT CHRIST

By this we know that we know Him, if we keep His commandments. Whoever keeps His word, truly the love of God is perfected in Him.

1 John 2:3, 5

Therefore, having been justified by faith, we have peace with God through our Lord Jesus Christ, through whom also we have access by faith into this grace in which we stand, and rejoice in hope of the glory of God. And not only that, but we also glory in tribulations, knowing that tribulation produces perseverance; and perseverance, character; and character, hope.

Romans 5:1–4

Be strong in the Lord and in the power of His might. Put on the whole armor of God, that you may be able to stand against the wiles of the devil.

Ephesians 6:10–11

# REFLECTING CHRIST

h, how steady, how consistent, how reliable is your Lord Jesus! His love is unchanging: Jeremiah 31:3. His Word is unchanging: 1 Peter 1:24-25. His throne is unchanging: Hebrews 1:8. His salvation is unchanging: Hebrews 7:24-25. His gifts to you are unchanging: James 1:17. He Himself is unchanging: Malachi 3:6.

And you want to be like Jesus. Do you sense that your life has a steadiness to it? Or do you want it to? What is it about your life that's up-and-down? . . .

Wherever in yourself you sense a tendency to instability, quickly reach to an outside source and deliberately build in accountability.

The point is, begin to mold your life to His; start to reflect Him. "Seek his face always" (Ps. 105:4). Soon you, too, will begin to project His kind of wonderful reliability, flow, steadiness, dependability, continuity.

Anne Ortlund
*Fix Your Eyes on Jesus*

# THE
# Joy
## OF PRAYING
## AND READING
## GOD'S WORD

*To walk with God, we must make it a practice to talk with God.*

Peninnah had children, but Hannah had no children. . . .

And [Hannah] was in bitterness of soul. And prayed to the LORD and wept in anguish. Then she made a vow and said, "O LORD of hosts, if You will indeed look on the affliction of Your maidservant and remember me, and not forget Your maidservant, but will give Your maidservant a male child, then I will give him to the LORD all the days of his life. . . ."

So it came to pass in the process of time that Hannah conceived and bore a son, and called his name Samuel, saying, "Because I have asked for him from the LORD." . . .

Now when she had weaned him, she took him up with her . . . and brought him to the house of the LORD in Shiloh. And the child was young. . . . And she said, " . . . I am the woman who stood by you here, praying to the LORD. For this child I prayed, and the LORD has granted me my petition which I asked of Him. Therefore I also have lent him to the LORD; as long as he lives he shall be lent to the LORD."

🌿 1 Samuel 1:2, 10, 11, 20, 24–28

# $\mathcal{P}$ART FOUR:
# THE JOY OF PRAYING AND READING GOD'S WORD

 efore Hannah knew she was going to have a baby, she promised God that if she had a son, she would give him to the Lord. It is one thing to make a promise when you are empty. It is quite another matter to keep your promise when full. Mothering made the years slip by quickly, and soon Samuel was weaned and ready to be brought to the temple. Hannah faced a tough challenge of faith as she prepared to permanently drop off her son at Eli's Day and Night Care Center. Eli's wicked sons had marred his reputation as a father. How could she leave her precious Samuel with such a family?

The answer was in God! God would tend to her son. She had promised her son to God, not to Eli. She must have left Samuel's ears ringing with the sounds of his mother worshiping, not weeping.

Jan Carlberg
*The Hungry Heart*

# PROMISES TO HELP
# YOU PRAISE GOD

Sing to the LORD a new song,
And His praise in the assembly of Saints.

🖼 Psalm 149:1

Praise the LORD!
Oh, give thanks to the LORD, for He is good!
For His mercy endures forever.
Who can utter the mighty acts of the LORD?
Who can declare all His praise?

🖼 Psalm 106:1–2

From the rising of the sun to its going down
The LORD's name is to be praised.

🖼 Psalm 113:3

# PRAISING GOD

 he wisdom and doctrine of Scripture teach that the experience of celebrating God is the core of worship. It is the quintessence of praise and thanksgiving—the most perfect manifestation of a heart that gratefully fellowships with the One who provides life and all the gifts of living. In fact, a grateful heart is not only the greatest virtue, it is the seedbed for all other virtues.

When we are caught up in the celebration of God there is neither room nor time for the invasion of negative living. As we rejoice before the Lord, as we serve Him in the area of our calling, as we enter into the love that surrounds our days, as we give thanks to Him for His kindness and faithfulness, we celebrate God.

Luci Swindoll
*You Bring the Confetti*

# PROMISES ABOUT THE JOY OF SOLITUDE AND SILENCE

Meditate within your heart . . . and be still.
Offer the sacrifices of righteousness,
And put your trust in the LORD.

Psalm 4:4–5

*Be still, and know that I am God;*
*I will be exalted among the nations,*
*I will be exalted in the earth!*

Psalm 46:10

The LORD is good to those who wait for Him,
To the soul who seeks Him.
It is good that one should hope and
    wait quietly
for the salvation of the LORD.

Lamentations 3:25–26

# SEEKING SOLITUDE
# AND SILENCE

 he ancient Desert Fathers used to commit themselves to a disciplinary creed: silence, solitude, and inner peace (*fuge, tace, et quiesce*). Only after adequate amounts of time listening, did they consider themselves ready to speak. . . .

Among many Christian women today, there is a strange sort of logic that suggests that spiritual resource and renewal are found in constantly seeking new voices, attending more meetings, listening to incessant music, and gathering to exchange half thought-out opinions. How often do we fall into the trap of believing that God is most pleased when we have maximized our information, our schedules, our relationships? . . .

Disengagement means silence before God, first of all. It is a time of heavenly discussion during which we listen more than we speak. And silence demands solitude.

Gail MacDonald
*High Call, High Privilege*

# PROMISES TO HELP YOU TRUST GOD

*It shall come to pass*
*That before they call, I will answer;*
*And while they are still speaking,*
*    I will hear.*

■ Isaiah 65:24

You will keep him in perfect peace,
Whose mind is stayed on You,
Because he trusts in You.
Trust in the LORD forever,
For in YAH, the LORD, is everlasting strength.

■ Isaiah 26:3–4

Behold, God is my salvation,
I will trust and not be afraid;
For YAH, the LORD, is my strength and song;
He also has become my salvation.

■ Isaiah 12:2

# TRUSTING GOD

hether it's a financial crunch, a sudden illness, or a personal defeat, if you fix your heart on praise to God, then you have offered a sacrifice. If you've ever cried during those heartbreaking difficulties, "Lord, I will hope in You and praise You more and more," then you know you have offered words that have cost you plenty. Praise in those circumstances is painful. . . .

I've been told that the Hebrew word for *awaiting* means "quiet trust." Those words don't sparkle with effervescence. It's like saying, "I have prayed about this burden, and now, Lord, I will quietly wait on You even before I see the answer. I expect it. And this is my sacrifice of praise to You—I believe and trust."

Please remember this: Most of the verses written about praise in God's Word were voiced by people faced with crushing heartaches, injustice, treachery, slander, and scores of other difficult situations. They knew that the sacrifice of praise was a key to victory on their spiritual journey.

Joni Eareckson Tada
*Seeking God*

# PROMISES ABOUT WORSHIPING GOD

Give unto the LORD, O you mighty ones,
Give unto the LORD glory and strength.
Give unto the LORD the glory due to His name;
Worship the LORD in the beauty of holiness.

Psalm 29:1–2

Oh come, let us worship and bow down;
Let us kneel before the LORD our Maker.
For He is our God,
And we are the people of His pasture,
And the sheep of His hand.

Psalm 95:6–7

The hour is coming, and now is, when the true worshipers will worship the Father in spirit and truth; for the Father is seeking such to worship Him. God is Spirit, and those who worship Him must worship in spirit and truth.

John 4:23–24

# Worshiping God

 ou've looked through a toy kaleidoscope, and as you twisted the tube, the bits of colored glass kept repatterning over and over. Look at Jesus Christ to see God's glory, and that glory will be "new every morning," always different, always beautiful. . . .

You're looking through the kaleidoscope at Jesus Christ, "the radiance of God's glory." Twist the tube a little. Oh—He's the Lord, transfigured before Peter, James, and John. His face shines like the sun, and His clothes become as white as the light . . . Twist the tube. Oh—He is the compassionate God. Two blind men are before Him, begging, "Lord, we want our sight." And Jesus touches their eyes and they see. . . . Twist the tube. "Abounding in love and faithfulness". Now He's feeding the five thousand hungry people. Twist . . . "Gracious": He's taking children into His arms . . . Keep twisting and twisting, and every time you stop, you'll see another radiant facet of the glory of God.

Anne Ortlund
*Fix Your Eyes on Jesus*

# PROMISES TO KEEP YOUR FOCUS ON GOD

In returning and rest you shall be saved;
In quietness and confidence shall be
your strength.

*Isaiah 30:15*

The works of the LORD are great,
Studied by all who have pleasure in them.
His work is honorable and glorious,
And His righteousness endures forever.
He has made His wonderful works to be
remembered.
The LORD is gracious and full of compassion.

*Psalm 111:3–4*

So we are always confident, knowing that
while we are at home in the body we are
absent from the Lord. For we walk by faith, not
by sight.

*2 Corinthians 5:6–7*

# FOCUSING ON GOD

rayer is not merely going to God with a shopping list of things we want Him to do for us and for our families. Rather, it is being in relationship with Him, listening to Him, and sharing our hearts with Him. . . .

We must remember *who* it is that we are talking with—the Almighty God. I have found it helpful to begin and end my prayers by focusing on His character traits. He is the Almighty God. He is the God who heals. He is the God of peace. He is the God who forgives. He is the God who provides, and He is the God who is in control. He knows everything that is happening. He is not caught off guard. His love is perfect.

As I consider *who* He is instead of focusing on myself or another person or my situation, I am better able to pray with faith. When I look at what God has to work with—me, my mate, my child, or my extended family   my expectations can be small, but when I focus on who He is, it is easier to believe.

Susan Alexander Yates
*A House Full of Friends*

# PROMISES ABOUT ASKING HARD QUESTIONS

For we do not have a High Priest who cannot sympathize with our weaknesses, but was in all points tempted as we are, yet without sin. Let us therefore come boldly to the throne of grace, that we may obtain mercy and find grace to help in time of need.

🔖 Hebrews 4:15–16

I know the thoughts that I think toward you, says the LORD, thoughts of peace and not of evil, to give you a future and a hope. Then you will call upon Me and go and pray to Me, and I will listen to you. And you will seek Me and find Me, when you search for Me with all your heart.

🔖 Jeremiah 29:11–13

*He who gets wisdom loves his own soul;*
*He who keeps understanding will*
*find good.*

🔖 Proverbs 19:8

# ASKING HARD QUESTIONS

n reading the book of Job . . . I [am] comforted that Job could not simply settle for the long-accepted religious answers when they did not make sense with his experience. When the atrocities of his physical condition worsened and the taunting of his comforters seemed never-ending, he chose to take both his experience and his questions and argue them before God. Even in the midst of his pain and confusion and despair, even under the silence of heaven, Job never trifled with the hopelessness of shutting God out. For whatever he did not understand about what was happening to him and why God had let it happen, he still trusted God enough to say, "Though he slay me, yet will I hope in him" (Job 13:15).

Verdell Davis
*Riches Stored in Secret Places*

# PROMISES ABOUT PRAYING FOR GOD'S WORK

You are of God, little children, and have overcome them, because He who is in you is greater than he who is in the world.

🔹 1 John 4:4

And take the helmet of salvation, and the sword of the Spirit, which is the word of God; praying always with all prayer and supplication in the Spirit, being watchful to this end with all perseverance and supplication for all the saints.

🔹 Ephesians 6:17–18

Rejoice always, pray without ceasing, in everything give thanks; for this is the will of God in Christ Jesus for you.

🔹 1 Thessalonians 5:16–18

# PRAYING FOR GOD'S WORK

 od has given us prayer to have a realistic "work" that can be done in prison, in a wheel chair, in bed in a hospital or a hovel or a palace, on the march, in the midst of battle . . . , out on a Villars street as skiers are pushing and shoving past, or in the dark of a chalet when everyone else is asleep. We can have a practical, realistic part in the battle between God and Satan.

Astonishing? Unbelievable? But true. In Ephesians 6:10–20, the whole point is that the "armor of God" is needed to stand against, to wrestle against the "wiles of the devil." And it is there, in that context, that we are commanded to "pray always with all prayer and supplication in the Spirit." Prayer is not just icing on the cake of a so-called spiritual life; prayer is warm, close communication with the living God, and also a matter of doing an active *work* on His side of the battle.

Edith Schaeffer
*The Tapestry*

# PROMISES ABOUT MOVING GOD THROUGH PRAYER

Now this is the confidence that we have in
Him, that if we ask anything according to His
will, He hears us. And if we know that He hears
us, whatever we ask, we know that we have
the petitions that we have asked of Him.

*1 John 5:14–15*

Give ear, O LORD, to my prayer;
And attend to the voice of my supplications.
In the day of my trouble I will call upon You,
For You will answer me.

*Psalm 86:6–7*

The LORD has heard the voice of my weeping,
The LORD has heard my supplication;
The LORD will receive my prayer.

*Psalm 6:8–9*

# MOVING GOD THROUGH PRAYER

 t's been said that faith may move mountains, but prayer moves God. Amazing, isn't it, that our prayers, whether grand and glorious or feeble and faint, can move the very heart of God who created the universe? To walk with God we must make it a practice to talk with God. . . .

Prayer moves God, and when God moves in your life, things get exciting! Years ago I never dreamed that God would move in my life the way He has. Even after my accident, when I signed up at the University of Maryland for art and English classes, I never realized how God would use diverse elements in my life to mold me to His will. But I sensed God was preparing me for something, and He started me out on a spiritual journey of prayer and praise that has not yet ended. You, too, have a journey through life ahead. Why not make it a journey of prayer and praise?

Joni Eareckson Tada
*Seeking God*

# PROMISES TO HELP
# YOU PRAY DAILY

Evening and morning and at noon
I will pray, and cry aloud,
And He shall hear my voice.

❦ Psalm 55:17

In his upper room, with his windows open
toward Jerusalem, [Daniel] knelt down on his
knees three times that day, and prayed and
gave thanks before His God, as was his
custom since early days.

❦ Daniel 6:10

Seven times a day I praise You,
Because of Your righteous judgments.

❦ Psalm 119:164

# $\mathscr{P}$RAYING DAILY

 rayer is sort of like an unlocked door with a giant, red-lettered sign on it that says: "Welcome. Feel Free to Take Whatever You Need." Inside is the storehouse of all that God is. He invites us to share it all. He doesn't intend for us to stay on the outside and struggle all alone with the perplexities of life, and He not only invites us to come in but to stay in, in order that His "Grace and peace be *yours in fullest measure,* through the knowledge of God and Jesus our Lord" (2 Pet. 1:2, NEB, emphasis mine). . . .

It is an ongoing process, not just an occasional religious-sounding speech we make to a nebulous divinity "out there somewhere." Prayer is meant to be a part of our lives, like breathing and thinking and talking.

Gloria Gaither
*Decisions*

# PROMISES ABOUT GAINING PERSPECTIVE FROM GOD'S WORD

I will meditate on Your precepts,
And contemplate Your ways.
I will delight myself in Your statutes;
I will not forget Your word.

Psalm 119:15–16

Your word is a lamp to my feet
And a light to my path.

Psalm 119:105

So then faith comes by hearing, and hearing by the word of God.

Romans 10:17

But these are the ones sown on good ground, those who hear the word, accept it, and bear fruit; some thirtyfold, some sixty, and some a hundred.

Mark 4:20

# GAINING PERSPECTIVE FROM GOD'S WORD

he Bible is a remarkable commentary on perspective. Through its divine message we are brought face to face with issues and tests in daily living and how, by the power of the Holy Spirit, we are enabled to respond positively to them. In that timeless volume we read about things that happen in our twentieth-century world. From its pages we are instructed how to cope with or react to our problems in the proper perspective.

It addresses issues involving humility, waiting, suffering, self-centeredness, loss, adversity, prosperity, loneliness, fear, . . . all of the things that get us down. Without this perspective, we make ourselves (and everybody else) miserable because we think we are the apex upon which the world turns. We think the sun rises and sets in our coming and going. Generally, when we live out our lives in that cocoon we are not only a disappointment and a trial to be with, but we are impoverished and ineffectual as well. The proper perspective creates within us a spirit of reaching outside of ourselves with joy and enthusiasm.

Luci Swindoll
*You Bring the Confetti*

# PROMISES ABOUT BEING REFRESHED BY GOD'S WORD

How sweet are Your words to my taste,
Sweeter than honey to my mouth.

🕮 Psalm 119:103

The law of the LORD is perfect, converting
the soul;
The testimony of the LORD is sure, making wise
the simple;
The statutes of the LORD are right, rejoicing
the heart;
The commandment of the LORD is pure,
enlightening the eyes;
More to be desired are they than gold,
Yea, than much fine gold,
Sweeter also than honey and the honeycomb.

🕮 Psalm 19:7–8, 10

This Book of the Law, shall not depart from
your mouth, but you shall meditate in it
day and night, that you may observe to do
according to all that is written in it. For then
you will make your way prosperous, and
then you will have good success.

🕮 Joshua 1:8

# REFRESHED BY GOD'S WORD

he refreshing wet face cloth, hot or cold, that is handed to us in a Hong Kong restaurant, or at the end of a Swiss air flight, to help us get on with the next few minutes at the end of a tiring day, or a long voyage, accomplishes the same kind of physical wake-up jolt that we so often need intellectually, emotionally, psychologically, and spiritually. The Bible frequently hands us the refreshing wet face cloth to awaken us for today and remind us of the importance of what is at hand.

Edith Schaeffer
*The Tapestry*

# PROMISES ABOUT BEING GUIDED BY GOD'S WORD

Your word I have hidden in my heart,
That I might not sin against You.
Blessed are You, O LORD!
Teach me Your statutes.

Psalm 119:11–12

Be diligent to present yourself approved to
God, a worker who does not need to be
ashamed, rightly dividing the word of truth.

2 Timothy 2:15

The commandment is a lamp,
And the law is light;
Reproofs of instruction are the way of life.

Proverbs 6:23

# GUIDED BY GOD'S WORD

or as long as I can remember the Word of God has been the place for me to go for answers and direction— my fundamental guide in making decisions. It was where my family went when others brought us the broken pieces of their lives to be mended and healed. When parents came to the parsonage brokenhearted over a rebellious son or daughter, Daddy would open the Bible and read from the fifteenth chapter of Luke the story of the Prodigal—the wayward son who one day felt his father's love reaching all the way to the pigpen he had made of his life. "There's hope. Keep on loving," Daddy would say. . . .

Now as an adult I find the Bible is truly the "operations manual" for the construction and maintenance of my life. In our home, in our marriage, in our professional life, in our businesses, Bill and I are constantly faced with increasingly difficult choices. It is the Bible that we find speaks again and again to give us direction and help.

Gloria Gaither
*Decisions*

FINDING
Joy
IN HOPE,
COURAGE,
AND COMFORT

From the winds and rains of adversity
comes abundant growth and a beautiful life.

So Abraham rose early in the morning, and took bread and a skin of water; and putting it on her shoulder, he gave it and the boy to Hagar, and sent her away. Then she departed and wandered in the Wilderness of Beersheba. And the water in the skin was used up, and she placed the boy under one of the shrubs. Then she went and sat down across from him at a distance of about a bowshot; for she said to herself, "Let me not see the death of the boy." So she sat opposite him, and lifted her voice and wept.

And God heard the voice of the lad. Then the angel of God called to Hagar out of heaven, and said to her, "What ails you, Hagar? Fear not, for God has heard the voice of the lad where he is. Arise, lift up the lad and hold him with your hand, for I will make him a great nation."

And God opened her eyes, and she saw a well of water. Then she went and filled the skin with water, and gave the lad a drink.

Genesis 21:14–19

# $\mathcal{P}$ART FIVE:
# FINDING JOY IN HOPE,
# COURAGE, AND COMFORT

agar the homeless and her son Ishmael present a stark portrait of despair and futility. They wandered in a desert, out of water and worse, out of hope. Who would hear the sobs and notice one little homeless family? "God heard the boy crying, and the angel of God called to Hagar . . . 'Do not be afraid. . . .' Then God opened her eyes and she saw a well of water" (Genesis 21:17–19). This was no mirage; this was a miracle handled by ministering angels of our loving Father God. They drank, and "God was with the boy as he grew up" (v. 20).

What is your desert of despair, your place of parched hopelessness? The God of Hagar and Ishmael sees and hears you in your desert. He waits to sustain and refresh you today with living water.

Jan Carlberg
*The Hungry Heart*

# PROMISES ABOUT GROWING THROUGH ADVERSITY

Beloved, do not think it strange concerning the fiery trial which is to try you, as though some strange thing happened to you; but rejoice to the extent that you partake of Christ's suffering.

1 Peter 4:12–13

Though I walk in the midst of trouble,
You will revive me;
You will stretch out Your hand
Against the wrath of my enemies,
And Your right hand will save me.

Psalm 128:7

Now thanks be to God who always leads us in triumph in Christ, and through us diffuses the fragrance of His knowledge in every place.

2 Corinthians 2:14

# GROWING THROUGH ADVERSITY

 hile spending time painting in the area of Italy known as Tuscany, I became accustomed to seeing grape vines growing on the hillsides. The older gnarled vines were beautiful to sketch because of their knotty twists and bends. Over the course of time, the winds, rains and sun—the weathering effects of the seasons—had forced their shapes. The most luscious growth came from these rugged old vines . . . grapes so heavy and bountiful they seemed to invite people to pick them.

In another vineyard were young plants which had suffered no ill effects of nature at all. They offered no particular beauty or character and were hardly worthy of my pencil or paintbrush.

As it is in nature, so it is in God's kingdom. From the winds and rains of adversity comes abundant growth and a beautiful life worth painting.

Do not be afraid to suffer. . . . It is from being shaken apart and not being destroyed that one becomes strong and courageous.

Laura Lewis Lanier
*All Things Bright and Beautiful*

# PROMISES TO HELP YOU TRADE HURT FOR WHOLENESS

The LORD is near to those who have a
    broken heart,
And saves such as have a contrite spirit.
Many are the afflictions of the righteous,
But the LORD delivers him out of them all.

🕮 Psalm 34:18–19

Come to Me, all you who labor and are heavy
laden, and I will give you rest. Take My yoke
upon you and learn from Me, for I am gentle
and lowly in heart, and you will find rest for
your souls.

🕮 Matthew 11:28–29

And the ransomed of the LORD shall return,
And come to Zion with singing,
With everlasting joy on their heads.
They shall obtain joy and gladness,
And sorrow and sighing shall flee away.

🕮 Isaiah 35:10

# TRADING HURT
# FOR WHOLENESS

 e live in a world gone wrong, one that was created perfect but now suffers the ravages of sin: death, violated relationships, children born with disabilities and deformities, disease, man's inhumanity to man, moral failures, tragedies of major proportions, chaos. It is, indeed, a broken world. But it is one thing to shake our heads at the mess the world is in; it is quite another to confront the reality of it in our own lives. One layer away, it is sad. But when it hits us, it is ominous. . . .

When we stand in the middle of a lifestorm, it seems as if the storm has become our way of life. We cannot see a way out. We are unable to chart a course back to smoother waters. We feel defeated—and broken. Will that brokenness produce a cynicism that will keep us forever in the mire of "if only" thinking? Or will we yield up that brokenness to the resources of One who calms the winds and the waves, heals the brokenhearted, and forgives the most grievous of sins? The choice is ours.

Verdell Davis
*Riches Stored in Secret Places*

# PROMISES ABOUT
# HOPING IN GOD

You shall eat in plenty and be satisfied,
And praise the name of the LORD your God,
Who has dealt wondrously with you;
And My people shall never be put to shame.

🌑 Joel 2:26

For I am persuaded that neither death nor life,
nor angels nor principalities nor powers, nor
things present nor things to come, nor height
nor depth, nor any other created thing, shall be
able to separate us from the love of God which
is in Christ Jesus our Lord.

🌑 Romans 8:38–39

Oh the depth of the riches both of the
wisdom and knowledge of God! How
unsearchable are His judgments and His ways
past finding out!

🌑 Romans 11:33

# HOPING IN GOD

 hen our "hope is built on nothing less than Jesus' blood and righteousness," as one of my favorite old hymns states, the desire and expectation of this fulfillment can never disappoint us. It is only our own dreams, ideas, and plans that are outside God's desires for us that cause us to lose hope and be disappointed.

Hope and new beginnings are fresh every morning. It is not necessary to wait for a circumstance to bring hope. Hope, real hope, comes when we lay down our own ideas and plans . . . our mind, will and emotions . . . before God as a hand of cards dealt and say to Him, "How would YOU play them?"

Laura Lewis Lanier
*All Things Bright and Beautiful*

# PROMISES ABOUT STRUGGLING THROUGH HEARTACHE

The LORD also will be a refuge for the oppressed,
A refuge in times of trouble.
And those who know Your name will put their
    trust in You;
For You, LORD, have not forsaken those who
    seek You.

*Psalm 9:9–10*


*In the day when I cried out,*
    *You answered me,*
*And made me bold with strength*
    *in my soul.*

*Psalm 138:3*


The LORD will guide you continually,
And satisfy your soul in drought,
And strengthen your bones;
You shall be like a watered garden,
And like a spring of water, whose waters
    do not fail.

*Isaiah 58:11*

# STRUGGLING THROUGH HEARTACHE

 have yet to meet a humorist, a comedian, or a clown who didn't have some deep hurt at the heart of his or her humor. When we laugh at something, we are in essence saying, "I identify with that!" If someone stood up and described all their blessings, we would be disgusted. When they stand up and share all their faults and foibles, we laugh and love them for it. Rosita Perez kindly encouraged me in a letter with these words: "Whoever says laughter isn't healing just hasn't hurt enough."

Laughter does not mean you are ignoring pain, living in denial, or just not aware of the troubles around you. . . . For me, laughter is how we take a much-needed break from the heartache, such that when we turn to face it again, it has by some miracle grown smaller in size and intensity, if not disappeared altogether.

Liz Curtis Higgs
*Only Angels Can Wing it*

# PROMISES TO HELP YOU BE STRONG IN THE BROKEN PLACES

*My heart is steadfast, O God,*
*my heart is steadfast;*
*I will sing and give praise.*

Psalm 57:7

And He said to me, "My grace is sufficient for you, for My strength is made perfect in weakness." Therefore most gladly I will rather boast in my infirmities, that the power of Christ may rest upon me.

2 Corinthians 12:9

The LORD will perfect that which concerns me; Your mercy, O LORD, endures forever; Do not forsake the works of Your hands.

Psalm 138:8

# BECOMING STRONG
# IN THE BROKEN PLACES

o become strong in the broken places in our lives demands that we do two things, seeming opposites: hang in there, and let go. To somehow dig up the courage to keep going is the very courage that allows us to scoop up the broken pieces of our lives and lay them all at the feet of One who would do more in us than just get us through the storm. As James Means said, he would take the fire that blackens our horizons and warm our souls with it. He would sharpen our vision in the darkness that oppresses us. He would use the despair of standing at a grave to deepen our trust. This we cannot do for ourselves.

Perhaps because our brokenness brings us to the end of ourselves, it is here, in these jars of clay that we offer up to his very special grace, that God's all-surpassing power is made known and he, indeed, makes us strong in our broken places.

Verdell Davis
*Riches Stored in Secret Places*

# PROMISES TO HELP WHEN YOU WALK THROUGH DEEP WATERS

When you pass through the waters,
    I will be with you;
And through the rivers, they will not
    overflow you.
When you walk through the fire, you shall
    not be burned;
Nor shall the flame scorch you.

        Isaiah 43:2

Though I walk through the valley of the
shadow of death,
I will fear no evil;
For You are with me;
Your rod and Your staff, they comfort me.

        Psalm 23:4

You number my wanderings;
Put my tears into Your bottle;
Are they not in Your book?
In God I have put my trust;
I will not be afraid.
What can man do to me?

        Psalm 56:8, 11

# Walking through
# Deep Waters

ll God's children go through deep
waters and trials by fire. There's no
if—only when. But with the *when*
comes a *Who*. God never allows His
children to swim alone. His buddy system is
sink-and-fire-proof. More sure than the *when*
is the *Who*. It is God who assures His children,
"*I will be with you*"—when!

Can you see God in your trials by water or
fire? God says to you, "I will be with you
whenever, wherever, and forever."

Jan Carlberg
*The Hungry Heart*

# PROMISES ABOUT SEEKING SHELTER IN GOD

*Keep me as the apple of Your eye;*
*Hide me under the shadow of*
    *Your wings.*

                Psalm 17:8

He raises the poor out of the dust,
And lifts the needy out of the ash heap,
He grants the barren woman a home,
Like a joyful mother of children.

                Psalm 113:7, 9

In the time of trouble
He shall hide me in His pavilion;
In the secret place of His tabernacle
He shall hide me;
He shall set me high upon a rock.

                Psalm 27:5

# SEEKING SHELTER IN GOD

 ome Christians treat God as a kind of insurance agent. In hard times, they expect Him to issue a claim check to restore what they've lost. While waiting for Him to change their circumstances for the better, they withhold fellowship from Him. Life's "squeeze" reveals their lack of submission and stubborn attitudes.

It is the heaven-born instinct of a child of God to seek shelter beneath the wings of the Almighty. The tendency to complain or to assert that God owes us something is not spiritual.

The godly instinct of a child of God is to say with Job, "Oh, that I might find Him."

Joni Eareckson Tada
*Seeking God*

# PROMISES TO HELP
# YOU WAIT PATIENTLY

My soul waits for the Lord
More than those who watch for the morning—
Yes, more than those who watch for the
    morning.

⬛ Psalm 130:6

My brethren, count it all joy when you fall
into various trials, knowing that the testing of
your faith produces patience. But let patience
have its perfect work, that you may be perfect
and complete, lacking nothing.

⬛ James 1:2–4

Therefore, be patient brethren, until the
coming of the Lord. See how the farmer waits
for the precious fruit of the earth, waiting
patiently for it until it receives the early and
latter rain. You also be patient.

⬛ James 5:7–8

# Waiting Patiently

ometimes it's hard to explain hope—just what is hope, anyway? The cutest illustration of hope I've found is about a little boy who was standing at the foot of the escalator in a big department store, intently watching the handrail. He never took his eyes off the handrail as the escalator kept going around and around. A salesperson saw him and finally asked him if he was lost. The little fellow replied, "Nope. I'm just waiting for my chewing gum to come back."

If your face is in the dust, if you are in a wringer situation, be like the little boy waiting for his chewing gum to come back. Stand firm, be patient, and trust God. Then get busy with your life . . . there is work to do.

Barbara Johnson
*Stick a Geranium in Your Hat
and Be Happy*

# PROMISES TO HELP YOU FIND SAFETY IN GOD

I will both lie down in peace, and sleep;
For You alone, O LORD, make me dwell in safety.

🔖 Psalm 4:8

*I will dwell in them and walk among them,
I will be their God, and they shall be
My people.*

🔖 2 Corinthians 6:16

The LORD our God is He who brought us and
our fathers up out of the land of Egypt, from
the house of bondage, who did those great
signs in our sight, and preserved us in all the
way that we went and among all the people
through whom we passed.

🔖 Joshua 24:17

# FINDING SAFETY IN GOD

ay by day, morning by morning, begin your walk with Him in the calm trust that God is at work in everything. George Mueller used to say, "It is my first business every morning to make sure that my heart is happy in God." He was right! It is your personal business, as a discipline of your heart, to learn to be peaceful and safe in God in every situation.

Some of my mornings I read this, written in my notebook:

The light of God surrounds me;

The love of God enfolds me;

The power of God protects me;

The presence of God watches over me;

Wherever I am, God is.

Remember, friend, where your real living is going on. In your thinking, in your reacting, in your heart of hearts—here is where your walk with God begins and continues. So when you start to move into trusting Him, stay there. Don't wander out again into worry and doubt!

Anne Ortlund
*Disciplines of the Heart*

# PROMISES ABOUT
# RECEIVING GOD'S COMFORT

Have I not commanded you? Be strong
and of good courage; do not be afraid, nor be
dismayed, for the LORD your God is with you
wherever you go.

Joshua 1:9

Hear my cry, O God;
Attend to my prayer.
From the end of the earth I will cry to You,
When my heart is overwhelmed;
Lead me to the rock that is higher than I.

Psalm 61:1

Be merciful to me, O Lord,
for I cry to You all day long.
Rejoice the soul of Your servant,
for to You, O Lord, I lift up my soul.

Psalm 86:3–4

# RECEIVING GOD'S COMFORT

This year as I once again looked forward to celebrating Christmas Eve, I paused to reflect. All the preparations for the traditional Swedish smorgasbord were completed except for the final serving of the dishes, which ranged from pickled herring and potato sausage to the Christmas cookies, cut into their various festive shapes and sprinkled with colored sugar.

Red candles were lighted all over the house, and in its usual place in the dining room stood my little tree with its colored lights which my father bought me when I was four. . . . Even on the Christmas that fell a week after my father was buried, . . . small gifts shared with family and friends provided the comfort of the familiar and reminded all of us of the true meaning of Christmas. . . . My father had joined the great cloud of witnesses in Heaven. His last words on this earth which were known to us were, "It is the grace of God which has brought me this far, and it is the grace of God which will bring me through." Those words in themselves were a comfort.

Elizabeth Skoglund
*Safety Zones*

# PROMISES ABOUT GOD'S FAITHFULNESS

*T*herefore know that the LORD your God, He is God, the faithful God who keeps covenant and mercy for a thousand generations with those who love Him and keep His commandments.

Deuteronomy 7:9

*M*ercy shall be built up forever;
Your faithfulness You shall establish in the
very heavens.

Psalm 89:2

*G*od is faithful, by whom you were called into the fellowship of His Son, Jesus Christ our Lord.

1 Corinthians 1:9

# REMEMBERING GOD'S FAITHFULNESS

o most of us who live in northern climates, spring seems to follow winter at a snail's pace. But eventually flowers peek through chilled soil and bird songs replace the scrape of snowplows. Bulky coats and boots hide in closets or attics, and screens replace storm windows and doors. . . .

Eventually, in the heat of August, winter may even seem like a long overdue friend. But come next January, when spring hides like buried treasure, remember . . . as sure as winter came, it will eventually leave. The same holds true for the winter of the soul. One day God will surprise you with the sight and song of spring.

In the darkest winter God can surprise you with spring.

Jan Carlberg
*The Hungry Heart*

# PROMISES ABOUT RESTING IN GOD'S PEACE

Be anxious for nothing, but in everything by prayer and supplication, with thanksgiving, let your requests be made known to God; and the peace of God, which surpasses all understanding, will guard your hearts and minds through Christ Jesus.

Philippians 4:6–7

Peace I leave with you, My peace I give to you; not as the world gives do I give to you. Let not your heart be troubled, neither let it be afraid.

John 14:27

To those who are called, sanctified by God the Father, and preserved in Jesus Christ; mercy, peace, and love be multiplied to you.

Jude 2

# RESTING IN GOD'S PEACE

 oon after the Vietnam War ended the American Art Institute opened a contest asking people to send their artistic rendition of the meaning of peace. The institute received hundreds of paintings, most of them the kinds of things that typically depict calmness and tranquility. . . . In all, the responses were overwhelming in their portrayal of the kind of peacefulness we all desire.

However, in the painting the American Art Institute chose, the artist had captured a raging storm so vividly that, looking at it, you could almost hear the thunder. In the center of the picture was an open field, and there, nearly lost in the darkness of the clouds, the artist had painted a tree bowing to the strong winds. And in that tree was a nest where a mother bird hovered over her young. The one-word caption was simply: *Peace*.

That is the peace that "passes all understanding." It is peace in the midst of the storm, peace that comes with the cry, "Thy will, not mine, be done." Peace born of the assurance that we are not alone.

Verdell Davis
*Riches Stored in Secret Places*

# THE Joy OF GOD'S PLAN FOR YOUR LIFE

*God doesn't want you to live a mediocre life.*

*T*hen [Naomi] arose with her daughters-in-law
that she might return from the country of
Moab, for she had heard . . . that the LORD
had visited His people by giving them bread.
Therefore she went out from the place where
she was, and her two daughters-in-law with her;
and they went on the way to return to the land
of Judah. And Naomi said to her two daughters-
in-law, "Go return each to her mother's house.
The LORD deal kindly with you, as you have dealt
with the dead and with me. . . ."

   Then they lifted up their voices and wept
again; and Orpah kissed her mother-in-law, but
Ruth clung to her.

   And [Naomi] said, "Look, your sister-in-law
has gone back to her people and to her gods;
return after your sister-in-law."

   But Ruth said:
   "Entreat me not to leave you,
   Or to turn back from following after you;
   And wherever you lodge, I will lodge;
   Your people shall be my people,
   And your God my God."

                                    Ruth 1:6–8, 14–16

# $\mathcal{P}$ART SIX: THE JOY OF GOD'S PLAN FOR YOUR LIFE

o banners or bands welcomed Ruth when she arrived in Bethlehem. She had forsaken her familiar gods for the true God of Israel while living in Moab. . . . Yet, as a newcomer to faith and to fields of barley, Ruth found no manna or quail to feed her hunger, only fields to comb for small pickings. But Ruth did not glean unnoticed in a barley field in Bethlehem. God noticed her fresh faith in Him, her committed love for Naomi, and her willingness to glean instead of grumble, so He touched the heart of Boaz, who owned the field. How Boaz must have encouraged Ruth with his kindness and keen observations! God's wings—place of refuge for Ruth—hovered over Bethlehem, stirring up a harvest of blessings for an old and a young believer.

Will you believe that God sees you in your barley field, your place of difficult duty? God's blessings crop up even in barley fields!

Jan Carlberg
*The Hungry Heart*

# PROMISES ABOUT BLESSINGS IN YOUR DAILY TASKS

Commit your works to the LORD,
And your thoughts will be established.

*Proverbs 16:3*

This is the day the LORD has made;
We will rejoice and be glad in it.

*Psalm 118:24*

For we are His workmanship, created in Christ
Jesus for good works, which God prepared
beforehand that we should walk in them.

*Ephesians 2:10*

# BLESSINGS IN YOUR DAILY TASKS

nne Morrow Lindbergh observed somewhere in her timeless little book, *Gift from the Sea*, that most of us don't really mind pouring our lives out for a reason. What we do resent is the feeling that it is being dribbled away in small, meaningless drops for no good reason.

For me, one of the greatest frustrations of walking through the "dailiness" of my life as a Christian is that I don't always get to see how the bits and pieces of who I am fit into the big picture of God's plan. It's tempting at times to see my life as a meal here, a meeting there, a carpool, a phone call, a sack of groceries—all disjointed fragments of nothing in particular.

And yet I know I am called, as God's child, to believe by faith that they do add up. That in some way every single scrap of my life, every step and every struggle, is in the process of being fitted together into God's huge and perfect pattern for good.

Claire Cloninger
*When God Shines Through*

# PROMISES ABOUT PRODUCING FRUITS OF RIGHTEOUSNESS

*Let us hear the conclusion of the whole matter:*
*Fear God and keep His commandments,*
*For this is man's all.*

Ecclesiastes 12:13

That you may approve the things that are excellent, that you may be sincere and without offense till the day of Christ, being filled with the fruits of righteousness which are by Jesus Christ, to the glory and praise of God.

Philippians 1:10–11

But the fruit of the Spirit is love, joy, peace, longsuffering, kindness, goodness, faithfulness, gentleness, self-control. Against such there is no law.

Galatians 5:22

# PRODUCING FRUITS OF RIGHTEOUSNESS

 ost of us suffer from information overload. The media bombards us with data, instant replays, and unwanted analyses. Our desks, bulletin boards, computers, and refrigerators spit out or show up our "to do" lists. Yet most days leave us with the nagging suspicion that we have overlooked or left undone the most important tasks.

The author of Ecclesiastes simplifies his sayings and the purpose of life with one statement: "Fear God and keep his commandments, for this is the whole duty of man." Such a simple "to do" list produces more than an ordered desk or refrigerator; it produces fruits of righteousness in our lives.

Jan Carlberg
*The Hungry Heart*

# PROMISES TO HELP YOU IDENTIFY GOALS

I must work the works of Him who sent Me while it is day; the night is coming when no one can work.

🌸 John 9:4

The humble He guides in justice,
And the humble He teaches His way.

🌸 Psalm 25:9

Commit your way to the LORD,
Trust also in Him,
And He shall bring it to pass.

🌸 Psalm 37:3

# IDENTIFYING GOALS

 hether we are sizing up our lives in total or confronting a specific decision, our important first questions must be, "Where do I want to go?" "What are my objectives?" "What, ultimately, do I want to accomplish?"

Identifying our objectives can be a complex task. Often there is more than one objective. For the Christian, the ultimate objective might be to best serve God with our abilities and talents, or to become more like Jesus. These are long-range objectives, and they are of prime importance. Added to them may be other, short-term goals: to house or care for our families, to be good stewards of our finances, to finish a specific project or to mend a broken relationship. . . .

We human beings can be very clever at conning ourselves. We can rationalize even spiritualize almost anything. But, in the final analysis, what we think is most important is what we will choose, no matter what we tell ourselves or other people.

Gloria Gaither
*Decisions*

# PROMISES TO HELP YOU ACCOMPLISH GOALS

I do not count myself to have apprehended; but one thing I do, forgetting those things which are behind and reaching forward to those things which are ahead, I press toward the goal for the prize of the upward call of God in Christ Jesus.

Philippians 3:13–14

I have been crucified with Christ; it is no longer I who live, but Christ lives in me; and the life which I now life in the flesh I live by faith in the Son of God, who loved me and gave Himself for me.

Galatians 2:20–21

Now may the God of peace Himself sanctify you completely; and may your whole spirit, soul, and body be preserved blameless at the coming of our Lord Jesus Christ. He who calls you is faithful, who also will do it.

1 Thessalonians 5:23–24

# ACCOMPLISHING GOALS

h, the joy of accomplishment! Aim for a goal and stick to it. And when you reach that goal, the natural result is to celebrate. We like to finish things, don't we? And to absolutely know we've finished, there's nothing like beating the drums, popping the corks, throwing the confetti, and commemorating the victory. If we realize a celebration is down the road, it makes the road easier to travel. The tests along the way are easier to bear. Personally, I find I am more willing to defer rewards when I anticipate a big event at the end of the journey. That event serves as an incentive toward which I aim. It is part of the "spoils of victory."

I love that thought. Many a time it has kept me going when all other inducements were dropping by the wayside. People were no longer cheering me on. My initial enthusiasm was waning. I was tired or discouraged. . . .

Rewards are the touchstones in our lives physically, materially, academically, financially, and even spiritually. They affirm our growth and the alchemy of our hearts.

Luci Swindoll
*You Bring the Confetti*

# PROMISES TO HELP YOU LIVE ABOVE MEDIOCRITY

Come, and let us go up to the mountain
    of the LORD,
To the house of the God of Jacob; He will
    teach us His ways,
And we shall walk in His paths.

Isaiah 2:3

Fight the good fight of faith, lay hold on
eternal life, to which you were also called and
have confessed the good confession in the
presence of many witnesses.

1 Timothy 6:12

I have fought the good fight, I have finished
the race, I have kept the faith. Finally, there is
laid up for me the crown of righteousness,
which the Lord, the righteous Judge, will give to
me on that Day, and not to me only but also to
all who have loved His appearing.

2 Timothy 4:7–8

# LIVING ABOVE MEDIOCRITY

 f you haven't before, deep inside your heart begin to believe a daring truth: God doesn't want you to live a mediocre life. In fact, here's His flat-out goal for you:

That you may become blameless and pure, children of God without fault in a crooked and depraved generation, in which you shine like stars in the universe. (Phil. 2:15)

You don't have to "live grey," feeling dirty, unworthy, mediocre, unfulfilled, and guilty.

And, my friend, whatever God asks you to be, He enables you to be! Second Peter 1:3 says that His divine power has given you everything you need for life and godliness! He says that you may even "participate in the divine nature and escape the corruption in the world caused by evil desires" (2 Pet. 1:4).

Anne Ortlund
*Disciplines of the Heart*

# PROMISES ABOUT COUNTING YOUR BLESSINGS

Blessed be the God and Father of our
Lord Jesus Christ, who has blessed us
with every spiritual blessing in the
heavenly places in Christ.

🕮 Ephesians 1:3

O LORD, You are my God.
I will exalt You,
I will praise Your name,
For You have done wonderful things;
Your counsels of old are faithfulness and truth.

🕮 Isaiah 25:1

The blessing of the LORD makes one rich,
And He adds no sorrow with it.

🕮 Proverbs 10:22

# COUNTING YOUR BLESSINGS

t's so easy for us to be focused on the negatives and forget all about the positives. Recently a good bit of my jewelry was stolen from a hotel room. Obviously that didn't make me happy, and I was doing everything possible to try to find it. The local police came to take my report, and the hotel security people were doing all they knew to help me. They kept apologizing to me, but I said to them, "Well, it's just jewelry. I haven't been notified that any of my family is sick or has a problem; I still have good health. This won't change my life in any significant way. I have so much to be thankful for that I refuse to let this unfortunate incident get to me."

Have you learned to stop and count your blessings in the middle of a bad day? It is such a good way to get your perspective back.

Mary Whelchel
*How to Thrive from 9 to 5*

# PROMISES ABOUT CELEBRATING SUCCESS

She watches over the ways of her household,
And does not eat the bread of idleness.
Her children rise up and call her blessed;
Her husband also, and he praises her:
"Many daughters have done well,
But you excel them all."

🌟 Proverbs 31:27–29

Then Miriam . . . took the timbrel in her
hand . . . and answered them:
"Sing to the LORD,
For he has triumphed gloriously!
The horse and its rider
He has thrown into the sea!"

🌟 Exodus 15:20–21

Then the women said to Naomi, "Blessed
be the LORD, who has not left you this day
without a close relative; and may his name
be famous in Israel! And may he be to you
a restorer of life and a nourisher of your
old age. . . ."

🌟 Ruth 4:14–15

# CELEBRATING SUCCESS

 sn't "victory" a wonderful word? Especially when it applies in your own life? Victory has been defined as "achievement in a struggle against odds or difficulties." It means winning. Look for a minute at some of the occasions in your past where you've been victorious in a pursuit or struggle, and you celebrated when it was over (or should have if you didn't):

- Job promotions
- Graduation from school
- Losing weight
- Paying off a debt
- Starting a business
- Writing a book

There are dozens more victories in your life which you can name, too. Didn't you feel relieved and ecstatic at the same time once that specific goal was attained? You're a winner, a success, a victor!

Luci Swindoll
*You Bring the Confetti*

# PROMISES TO HELP YOU
# LAUGH AT YOURSELF

*A merry heart does good, like medicine,*
*But a broken spirit dries the bones.*

Proverbs 17:22

Then our mouth was filled with laughter,
And our tongue with singing. . . .
The LORD has done great things for us
And we are glad.

Psalm 126:2–3

Behold God will not cast away the
blameless. . . .
He will yet fill your mouth with laughing,
And your lips with rejoicing.

Job 8:20–21

# LAUGHING AT YOURSELF

t's healthy to be willing to laugh at yourself and make light of your shortcomings. We all have our quirks, so we shouldn't take ourselves too seriously. One of the best solutions I know for that is to take the "bunnyslipper approach," a philosophy of life we all need to practice.

A friend sent me a pair of bunny slippers, and every now and then I put them on, especially when I'm tempted to start thinking I'm important or "nearly famous." There's something about bunny slippers that keeps my perspective where it belongs, but in addition to that, my bunny slippers remind me that whatever happens doesn't have to get me down. I can still be a little silly and laugh and enjoy life. Pain dissolves, frustrations vanish, and burdens roll away when I have on my bunny slippers.

Barbara Johnson
*Mama, Get the Hammer!*

# PROMISES ABOUT DARING TO RISK

*E*ye has not seen, nor ear heard,
Nor have entered into the heart of man
The things which God has prepared for those
who love Him.

> 1 Corinthians 2:9

*T*hen Job answered the LORD and said:
"I know that You can do everything,
And that no purpose of Yours can be withheld
from You."

> Job 42:1–2

*T*hen Esther told them to reply to Mordecai:
"Go and gather all the Jews who are present in
Shushan, and fast for me; neither eat nor drink
for three days, night or day. My maids and I will
fast likewise. And so I will go to the king, which
is against the law; and if I perish, I perish!"

> Esther 4:15–16

# DARING TO RISK

 welling on the past—successes or failures—is a waste of energy and a sin against the Holy Spirit, whose work it is to call out the gifts we have and make of us all God wants us to be. Even failure can be the springboard to growth and discovery, so we should never allow the fear of it to keep us from daring to risk.

Part of life's great adventure is the growth process itself. There is wonderful freedom and joy in coming to recognize that the fun is in the becoming. As long as we live, we will never "arrive," but only discover new tracts of unexplored territory.

Gloria Gaither
*Decisions*

# PROMISES TO HELP YOU LIVE A POWERFUL LIFE

A woman who fears the LORD,
She shall be praised.
Give her of the fruit of her hands,
And let her own works praise her in the gates.

Proverbs 31:31

But we have this treasure in earthen vessels,
that the excellence of the power may be of
God and not of us.

2 Corinthians 4:7

For God has not given us a spirit of fear,
but of power and of love and of a sound mind.

2 Timothy 1:7

# LIVING A POWERFUL LIFE

 et the only measure of your expectations for yourself be the resurrection power of Jesus Christ.

Then you can live a truly powerful life—not because you're no longer weak, but because, being weak, you count on His power to work in you.

We had company for dinner the other night, and the two lamps flanking the couch wouldn't go on. . . . But after they'd left, Ray investigated and found the plug in the wall socket was sort of sagging out and had lost its connection.

Never mind your weaknesses; just make sure you're solidly connected, strongly "abiding in Him." Then expect the power of His resurrection to work in your life.

Anne Ortlund
*Fix Your Eyes on Jesus*

# FINDING
# Joy
## IN POSITIVE
## LIVING

*No matter how bad things are,*
*no one can force you to have a bad attitude.*

*N*ow Joshua the son of Nun sent out two men from Acacia Grove to spy secretly, saying, "Go, view the land, especially Jericho."

So they went, and came to the house of a harlot named Rahab, and lodged there. And it was told the king of Jericho, saying," Behold, men have come here tonight from the children of Israel to search out the country."

So the king of Jericho sent to Rahab, saying, "Bring out the men who have come to you, who have entered your house, for they have come to search out all the country."

Then the woman took the two men and hid them. . . . And as soon as those who pursued them had gone out, they shut the gate.

Now before they lay down, she came up to them on the roof, and said to the men: "I know that the LORD has given you the land. . . . Now therefore, I beg you, swear to me by the LORD, since I have shown you kindness, that you also will show kindness to my father's house . . . and deliver our lives from death."

🕮 Joshua 2:1–4, 7–9, 12–13

# $\mathscr{P}$ART SEVEN: FINDING JOY IN POSITIVE LIVING

or the LORD your God is God in heaven above and on the earth below." Joshua 2:11

These are strange words coming from a harlot in a heathen culture! Rahab's reception of Joshua's spies was not rooted in her profession but in her awareness of a world beyond the walls of Jericho.

As an inn keeper and prostitute she must have heard fearful whispers and brash denunciations of this foreign God and His miraculous deliverance of His children. While the other citizens of Jericho feared, Rahab formed her faith in the God of Israel. And so she risked her life to hide the spies, thus identifying herself with God's people. Such faith lifted Rahab to Faith's Hall of Fame in Hebrews 11:31, where we read, "By faith the prostitute Rahab, because she welcomed the spies, was not killed with those who were disobedient."

Jan Carlberg
*The Hungry Heart*

# PROMISES TO HELP
# YOU CHOOSE A
# POSITIVE ATTITUDE

Now may the God of hope fill you with
all joy and peace in believing, that you
may abound in hope by the power of the
Holy Spirit.

*Romans 15:13*

You shall go out with joy
And be led out with peace;
The mountains and the hills
Shall break forth into singing before you,
And all the trees of the field shall clap
    their hands.

*Isaiah 55:12*

And we know that all things work together for
good to those who love God, to those who are
the called according to His purpose.

*Romans 8:28*

# CHOOSING A
## POSITIVE ATTITUDE

our attitude is your choice. It always is. We live in an age that has developed the art of shifting blame to very high levels, and sometimes we get caught up in that same tendency. "Well, if you had my job you wouldn't be so positive." "If you had my kids, you wouldn't feel so good." "If only my boss were different, I could be a positive person." In other words, "My bad attitude is not my fault!"

The truth is, however, your attitude and mine are always our choice. No matter how bad things are, no one can force you to have a bad attitude if you don't want to, and no matter how good things are, no one can force you to have a good attitude if you don't want to. Now that should come as really good news because it says our attitudes don't have to be the victims of our circumstances or of other people. We choose our responses.

Mary Whelchel
*How to Thrive from 9 to 5*

# Promises about being refreshed by simplicity

He who loves his life will lose it, and he who hates his life in this world will keep it for eternal life.

🔲 John 12:25

Set your mind on things above, not on things on the earth.

🔲 Colossians 3:2

Command those who are rich in this present age not to be haughty, nor to trust in uncertain riches but in the living God, who gives us richly all things to enjoy. Let them do good, that they be rich in good works, ready to give, willing to share, storing up for themselves a good foundation for the time to come, that they may lay hold on eternal life.

🔲 1 Timothy 6:17–19

# REFRESHED BY SIMPLICITY

here is something about baking bread that brings me back to earth from all the stresses of everyday modern life. Maybe it's kneading the dough, in all its simplicity and physicalness, that helps the most in relaxing me. Maybe it's the time required to let the bread rise that forces me temporarily to slow down. But whatever it is, these "back to earth days" and baking bread in general have become for me a safety zone where I can take some time and gain a perspective on what I'm doing. It is as though my feet get firmly placed again on earth, and the problems of yesterday begin to look solvable. Afterwards, that which looked hopeless no longer seems so impossible, and that which seemed complex appears less so in the light of a new day.

Elizabeth Skoglund
*Safety Zones*

# PROMISES ABOUT
# SPEAKING WORDS
# OF WISDOM

A soft answer turns away wrath
But a harsh word stirs up anger.
The tongue of the wise uses knowledge rightly,
But the mouth of fools pours forth foolishness.

Proverbs 15:1–2

For we all stumble in many things. If anyone
does not stumble in word, he is a perfect man,
able also to bridle the whole body.

James 3:2

The heart of the wise teaches his mouth,
And adds learning to his lips.
Pleasant words are like a honeycomb,
Sweetness to the soul and health to the bones.

Proverbs 16:23–24

# Speaking Words
# of Wisdom

 ob's friends pelted him with unrelenting words. Like torrential rains on parched soil, their words gouged deep gullies. Job attempted to escape like a tired swimmer, only to be crushed with a fresh wave of words. His comforters rapped him with anger, guilt, idle chatter, ignorance, and faulty conclusions. And he remained crushed instead of wrapped in comfort.

Do your words rain down comfort? Love chooses to cover instead of condemn. Job's choice confronts us daily. Some people provoke us to exchange blow for blow, gossip for gossip, curse for curse, rebuke for rebuke. To speak as Job's comforters spoke requires no wisdom or strength from God. That kind of speech comes naturally. But if we choose to use our words to encourage and comfort, we will need supernatural strength.

God is ready when you are.

Jan Carlberg
*The Hungry Heart*

# PROMISES TO HELP YOU WAIT WITH HOPE

But those who wait on the LORD
Shall renew their strength;
They shall mount up with wings like eagles,
They shall run and not be weary,
They shall walk and not faint.

Isaiah 40:31

And we desire that each one of you show
the same diligence to the full assurance of
hope until the end, that you do not become
sluggish, but imitate those who through faith
and patience inherit the promises.

Hebrews 6:11–12

Wait on the LORD;
Be of good courage,
And He shall strengthen your heart;
Wait, I say, on the LORD!

Psalm 27:14

# WAITING WITH HOPE

 here are so many periods of "waiting" in life that make time seem long, while the rest of life flies! There is waiting to finish school, waiting for exam results, waiting for the wedding day to arrive, and waiting for the baby to take nine months to grow; there is waiting for a long illness to "break" and signs of recovery to be real; there is the waiting for that event all Christians most urgently desire (at least in most periods of their lives)—for Christ to return and restore the fallen world, giving us our new bodies to be His Bride, with only glory ahead and no waiting left.

That will be a fulfillment with no shadow of disappointment.

Edith Schaeffer
*The Tapestry*

# PROMISES ABOUT REFUSING MISERY

Though I walk in the midst of trouble,
You will revive me;
You will stretch out Your hand
Against the wrath of my enemies,
And Your right hand will save me.

*Psalm 138:7*

I will mention the lovingkindnesses
of the LORD
And the praises of the LORD,
According to all that the LORD has
bestowed on us.

*Isaiah 63:7a*

What shall we say to these things? If God is for us, who can be against us? He who did not spare His own Son, but delivered Him up for us all, how shall He not with Him also freely give us all things?

*Romans 8:31–32*

# REFUSING MISERY

ain is inevitable for all of us, but we have an option as to how we react to the pain. It is no fun to suffer; in fact, it can be awful. We are all going to have pain, but misery is optional. We can decide how we react to the pain that inevitably comes to us all.

Since learning that I have diabetes, I have read a dozen books and even watched some video tapes to learn all I could about how to cope with this chronic, debilitating disease. The most important thing I learned is that having a proper mental attitude works wonders. If you take care of yourself and do all the things that you must do to keep it in control so that it doesn't control you, you can live a happy, productive life.

Barbara Johnson
*Stick a Geranium in Your Hat*
*and Be Happy*

# PROMISES ABOUT ENCOURAGEMENT

If then you were raised with Christ, seek those things which are above, where Christ is, sitting at the right hand of God. Set your mind on things above, not on things on the earth.

Colossians 3:1–2

*You are my hiding place;*
*You shall preserve me from trouble;*
*You shall surround me with songs*
*of deliverance.*

Psalm 32:7

Do not fear, little flock, for it is your Father's good pleasure to give you the kingdom.

Luke 12:32

# ENCOURAGING YOURSELF

ne morning, I spent ten indulgent minutes reading a favorite book that had nothing to do with work, child raising, or getting "buns of steel." It was just for enjoyment, just for me. . . .

Sometimes we just need to encourage ourselves. I was delighted with the responses from women who have developed that strength of character that says, as Janet from Nebraska phrased it, "I'm okay the way I am." "I am not perfect, but there is nothing I want to change . . . right now!" admitted Sheila. Or, as JoAnne said, "Being forty, I finally like my character traits."

While we all long to remain flexible, if we've come to a place of peace and acceptance, the time for adapting and contorting may be over and the time for knowing and sharing our strength may be at hand.

Liz Curtis Higgs
*Only Angels Can Wing It*

# PROMISES TO HELP YOU FIND GOOD IN EVERY CIRCUMSTANCE

Now may our Lord Jesus Christ Himself, and our God and Father, who has loved us and given us everlasting consolation and good hope by grace, comfort your hearts and establish you in every good word and work.

2 Thessalonians 2:16–17

When a man's ways please the LORD, He makes even his enemies to be at peace with him.

Proverbs 16:7

Blessed are those who do His commandments, that they may have the right to the tree of life, and may enter through the gates into the city.

Revelation 22:14

# FINDING GOOD IN EVERY CIRCUMSTANCE

 t's not your circumstances that shape you. They are outside you and beyond you; they can't really touch you. It's how you react to your circumstances that shapes you. That's between your ears, and that affects the "real you."

And what controls your reactions? Abiding in Christ (John 15:4–10 KJV). Staying there.

Then what if you find, for instance, a lump in your breast? Of course you'll make a doctor's appointment immediately—but that's external. What happens within? Lord, nothing important has changed. You love me. Your eternal, perfect plans for me are continuing on schedule. I will praise You; I will worship You. I will rest in all You're continuing to do in my life.

Anne Ortlund
*Disciplines of the Heart*

# PROMISES TO HELP YOU SEEK POSITIVE SOLUTIONS

*Listen to counsel and receive instruction,*
*That you may be wise in your latter days.*

Proverbs 19:20

*I* considered all this in my heart, so that I could declare it all: that the righteous and the wise and their works are in the hand of God.

Ecclesiastes 9:1

*But* you are a chosen generation, a royal priesthood, a holy nation, His own special people, that you may proclaim the praises of Him who called you out of darkness into His marvelous light.

1 Peter 2:9

# SEEKING POSITIVE SOLUTIONS

hen we get up in the morning, we have just so much energy. We can spend that energy creatively, seeking positive solutions, or we can spend it dragging ourselves down with negative thinking. Either way, we may still be tired at the end of the day. But in the first instance, we will have accomplished something and made progress. In the other we will have plodded along and managed to make ourselves not only tired, but depressed as well!

Half the battle in solving problems is our attitude. We are not just pumping ourselves full of sunshine when we say, "Think YES!" How we think about a situation usually dictates the course we will take. And sometimes, when we get bogged down in all the tangle of detail, we need a friend who will help us think clearly about all aspects of the situation, refocusing our attention from the obstacles to the possibilities in striving for proper choices and desired goals.

Gloria Gaither
*Decisions*

# PROMISES ABOUT
# LAUGHTER AND JOY

So they sang praises with gladness, and they
bowed their heads and worshiped.

*2 Chronicles 29:30*

Again there shall be heard in this place . . .
the voice of joy and the voice of gladness . . .
the voice of those who will say:
"Praise the LORD of Hosts,
For the LORD is good,
For His mercy endures forever. . . ."

*Jeremiah 33:10–11*

*A merry heart makes a cheerful countenance.
But by sorrow of the heart the spirit
is broken.*

*Proverbs 15:13*

Happy are the people whose God is LORD!

*Psalm 144:5*

# LOOKING FOR LAUGHTER AND JOY

e can learn to look for laughter and joy in the many ordinary places where we go. When I go to our La Habra post office in the morning, the cement on the sidewalk outside is just plain blah gray. But if I go in the afternoon, when the sun hits it, the cement sparkles with a million transient diamonds! So, I usually go in the afternoon, looking for the joy that can bounce off that cement right into my life, to remind me of the sparkles all around us, if we are willing to look for them.

But I repeat, you have to LOOK for the joy. Look for the light of God that is hitting your life, and you will find sparkles you didn't know were there.

Barbara Johnson
*Stick a Geranium in Your Hat*
*and Be Happy*

# PROMISES TO HELP YOU CHANGE YOUR FOCUS

Who among all these does not know
That the hand of the LORD has done this,
In whose hand is the life of every living thing,
And the breath of all mankind?

Job 12:9–10

Charm is deceitful and beauty is passing,
But a woman who fears the LORD, she shall
be praised.

Proverbs 31:30

Looking unto Jesus, the author and finisher of
our faith, who for the joy that was set before
Him endured the cross, despising the shame,
and has sat down at the right hand of the
throne of God.

Hebrews 12:2

# CHANGING YOUR FOCUS

he dog has tracked Alpo all over the kitchen floor. Your husband has called to say he'll be late. The saucepans are boiling over, and the burning casserole is staining your oven. Teenagers are wrestling in the bedroom above your kitchen. Little wonder you stand there with the dish towel in your hand, droop-shouldered and dumbfounded, not knowing what to do.

What we need here is more than a prayer mumbled in obligation. . . . We need a different focus. . . .

Consider Jesus. He had one heavy cross to bear, but He fixed His sight on the joy before Him. And we are to do the same.

So what about the burning casserole, the dirty kitchen floor, and the screaming kids upstairs? They haven't changed. But your focus has. Don't gaze at your problems while you only glance at the Lord. Get life in focus. Gaze at the Lord— behold Him—and your problems won't cause you to grow weary and lose heart.

Joni Eareckson Tada
*Seeking God*

FINDING
*Joy*
IN CONTENTMENT
AND OBEDIENCE

*Perspective is all about how we choose to see things.*

*N*ow in the sixth month the angel Gabriel was sent by God to a city of Galilee named Nazareth, to a virgin betrothed to a man whose name was Joseph, of the house of David. The virgin's name was Mary. And having come in, the angel said to her, "Rejoice, highly favored one, the Lord is with you; blessed are you among women!"

But when she saw him, she was troubled at his saying, and considered what manner of greeting this was. Then the angel said to her, "Do not be afraid, Mary, for you have found favor with God. And behold, you will conceive in your womb and bring forth a son, and shall call His name Jesus."

*Luke 1:26–31*

# PART EIGHT: FINDING JOY IN CONTENTMENT AND OBEDIENCE

ary, the mother of Christ, best exemplified the model woman. She was young and must have possessed enormous inner strength. Imagine the trust she must have had in God in order to cooperate with such a miracle as the birth of Jesus. She must also have had great strength to accept the gossip, to affirm Joseph, and to keep the entire event and its origin a secret:

Mary kept all these things and pondered them in her heart. (Luke 2:19, KJV)

I am amazed when I think of Mary's performance! She played a crucial role in presenting the Messiah to the world, but she kept quiet about it. A woman like that grows and becomes useful, though not necessarily noticed. . . .

Somewhere in Mary's life she had also made a conscious habit of saying yes to God's love. No fists clenched, no drooping hands. She said:

I am the handmaid of the Lord; let it be to me according to your Word. (Luke 1:38)

Gail MacDonald
*High Call, High Privilege*

# PROMISES ABOUT LIVING IN OBEDIENCE

*Let us not grow weary while doing good, for in due season we shall reap if we do not lose heart.*

⬛ Galatians 6:9

*L*et your heart therefore be loyal to the LORD our God, to walk in His statutes and keep His commandments, as at this day.

⬛ 1 Kings 8:61

*T*he LORD has revealed our righteousness. Come and let us declare in Zion the work of the LORD our God.

⬛ Jeremiah 51:10

# LIVING IN OBEDIENCE

 love crisp, cold days when you can smell the smoke of a cherry-wood fire from a neighbor's chimney. . . . I love the smell of fresh, damp laundry that you hang outside on the line. . . .

In 2 Corinthians 2:14 Paul wrote, "But thanks be to God, who always leads us in triumphal procession in Christ and through us spreads everywhere the fragrance of the knowledge of him."

That idea was borrowed from the ancient Roman parades of triumph. The apostle Paul compared himself, first, to one of the prisoners led in long chains behind the conqueror's chariot: then, to a servant bearing incense; and lastly, to the incense itself that rose all along the procession of triumph.

Paul knew the power behind a sweet fragrance. It is as though he were saying, "I desire to live that I may perpetually remind God of the obedience, sacrifice, and devotion of the Lord Jesus. I want my words and deeds to bring to the mind of God those wonderful, similar memories of the earthly life of Jesus."

Joni Eareckson Tada
*Seeking God*

# PROMISES TO HELP YOU
# GAIN SELF-DISCIPLINE

Everyone who is called by My name,
Whom I have created for My glory;
I have formed him, yes, I have made him.

Isaiah 43:7

Walk in the Spirit, and you shall not fulfill the
lust of the flesh.

Galatians 5:16

If we died with Him, we shall also live
with Him.
If we endure, we shall also reign with Him.

2 Timothy 2:11–12

# GAINING SELF-DISCIPLINE

motions. Can you imagine a life without them? Sure, it may be easier, it may be less complicated, and it may be more efficient. But how dull, how colorless, how unexciting! Emotions are a gift from God. To refuse to recognize them severs us from living with the fullness that can be ours through Jesus Christ. . . .

Gaining self-discipline over our emotions does not mean repressing or ignoring them. Our emotions can be strong allies if we recognize them, work through what they mean to us, and then choose to act a certain way to bring about positive and healthy changes in our lives.

Kathy Babbitt
*Habits of the Heart*

# PROMISES ABOUT
# SLOWING LIFE DOWN

Who is like the LORD our God,
Who dwells on high,
Who humbles Himself to behold
The things that are in the heavens
and in the earth?

🔖 Psalm 113:5–6

I cried to the LORD with my voice,
And He heard me from His holy hill.
I lay down and slept;
I awoke, for the LORD sustained me.

🔖 Psalm 3:4–5

Surely goodness and mercy shall follow me
All the days of my life;
And I will dwell in the house of the LORD
Forever.

🔖 Psalm 23:6

# SLOWING LIFE DOWN

Is the pace of your life too fast? What is it that's driving you?

Is it perfectionism? That's pure ego. You'll self-destruct. Confess your perfectionism to God and ask Him for deliverance.

Is it desire for excellence "for the sake of your witness"? Whose excellence, yours or God's?

Is it pure social pressure? Maybe you need to say no to some activities that "everybody"—even Christians—are involved in. They're sapping more energy from you or more finances—than you can afford to lose.

Is it love of money? This is so serious it's frightening. Jesus says you cannot serve both God and money (Matt. 6:24); you must choose one or the other. Wrestle that one to the ground and have done with it forever!

It will take the discipline of your heart to shift down.

Anne Ortlund
*Disciplines of the Heart*

# PROMISES TO HELP YOU CHOOSE TRANQUILITY

Whatever things are true, whatever things are noble, whatever things are just, whatever things are pure, whatever things are lovely, whatever things are of good report, if there is any virtue and if there is anything praiseworthy—meditate on these things.

Philippians 4:8

Let not your heart be troubled; you believe in God, believe also in Me. In My Father's house are many mansions; if it were not so, I would have told you. I go to prepare a place for you. And if I go and prepare a place for you, I will come again and receive you to Myself; that where I am, there you may be also.

John 14:1–3

# CHOOSING TRANQUILITY

 an you even begin to think of the time, energy, and emotions you've wasted on the uncontrollable things in your life? I've certainly done my share of wishing, fretting, complaining, and trying to manipulate uncontrollable things and people. When I do that, I use up immense quantities of emotional energy for nothing when it could have been expended in a productive way . . .

Remember this: When the uncontrollable things or people in our lives are making us miserable, it is because we allow them to do that to us. They can't keep us on that roller coaster if we decide to get off. How do you get off? By choice, by a decision of your will, by much prayer, and by the power of God's Spirit within you. It takes determination on your part, but if you don't let God supply the power, you're not likely to be able to do it.

Mary Whelchel
*How to Thrive from 9 to 5*

# PROMISES TO HELP YOU
# FIND A GOOD BALANCE

*The fruit of the righteous is a tree of life,*
*And he who wins souls is wise.*

Proverbs 11:30

So speak and so do as those who will be
judged by the law of liberty. For judgment is
without mercy to the one who has shown no
mercy. Mercy triumphs over judgment.

James 2:12–13

Be sober, be vigilant; because your adversary
the devil walks about like a roaring lion, seeking
whom he may devour. Resist him, steadfast in
the faith.

1 Peter 5:8–9a

# FINDING A GOOD BALANCE

 few years after my mother died, I remembered more vividly the times in childhood when she had made gloomy days seem cheerful. When I was very small, rainy days always meant something special to do inside, such as new paper dolls or a coloring book. Later, when I was in school, I always knew that on a rainy day I would come home to the smell of cookies baking in the oven. . . .

I remembered, too, that in my childhood my mother had always balanced grief with comfort, pain with joy. . . . To compensate for my childhood illnesses, for example, she used to read me stories which made the afternoon fly, or she would show me how to knit doll clothes out of the scraps of yarn which she had saved in a worn, brocade knitting bag. . . .

Whatever the specific method used, my mother had learned, long before I knew her, how to balance pain with pleasure.

Elizabeth Skoglund
*Safety Zones*

# PROMISES ABOUT BEING CONTENT

Now godliness with contentment is great
gain. For we brought nothing into this world,
and it is certain we can carry nothing out.
And having food and clothing, with these
we shall be content.

1 Timothy 6:6–8

I know that whatever God does,
it shall be forever.
Nothing can be added to it,
And nothing taken from it.

Ecclesiastes 3:14

But the wisdom that is from above is first
pure, then peaceable, gentle, willing to yield,
full of mercy and good fruits, without partiality
and without hypocrisy.

James 3:17

# LEARNING TO BE CONTENT

 ontentment is a stranger to most of us. Like octopi we spend ourselves gathering goods, scrambling after promotions, and juggling to include one more handful. Eventually, we collapse with full hands and empty hearts.

The wealthiest man, King Solomon, probably wrote, "Better one handful with tranquility than two handfuls with toil and chasing after the wind." (Eccle. 4:6) Perhaps we would do well to listen.

What could you do with one free hand? A content heart keeps a free hand.

Jan Carlberg
*The Hungry Heart*

# PROMISES TO HELP YOU REFLECT CHRIST'S HUMILITY

*On this one I will look:*
*On him who is poor and of a*
*contrite spirit,*
*And who trembles at My word.*

Isaiah 66:2

Do not let your adornment be merely outward—arranging the hair, wearing gold, or putting on fine apparel—rather let it be the hidden person of the heart, with the incorruptible beauty of a gentle and quiet spirit, which is very precious in the sight of God.

1 Peter 3:3

By humility and the fear of the LORD
Are riches and honor and life.

Proverbs 22:4

# REFLECTING CHRIST'S HUMILITY

 t is fascinating to ponder the fact that two thousand years ago God Himself chose to live . . . outside of His own enormity and entered into our smallness.

Jesus certainly could have opted for the spiritual power play. He could have come swooping into our world in a lightning-driven chariot. He could have zapped entire cities with the snap of His fingers. Instead, He arrived in one of the most fragile and vulnerable packages in the world, the body of a newborn baby. He grew up in a middle-class family, learned a trade, went to temple like other Jewish boys, and didn't even begin His formal ministry until He was thirty years old. Then He set out on foot to cover a relatively small corner of the world. He spoke to a few thousand people (often one at a time), discipled a handful of followers, and died the death of a common criminal. Still, He was pleased enough with the results of His small-scope ministry to say from the cross, "It is finished."

Claire Cloninger
*When God Shines Through*

# PROMISES TO HELP YOU CHANGE YOUR OUTLOOK

In the fear of the LORD there is strong
     confidence,
And His children will have a place of refuge.
The fear of the LORD is a fountain of life,
To turn one away from the snares of death.

Proverbs 14:26–27

For My thoughts are not your thoughts,
Nor are your ways My ways," says the LORD.
"For as the heavens are higher than the earth,
So are my ways higher than your ways,
And My thoughts than your thoughts."

Isaiah 55:8–9

For the LORD is a sun and shield;
The LORD will give grace and glory;
No good thing will He withhold
From those who walk uprightly.

Psalm 84:11

# CHANGING YOUR OUTLOOK

pportunities come in all shapes and sizes. What if those things you see now as obstacles could be seen instead as GOLD BRICKS? Bricks can be used to build a wall or as paving stones for your road to success. You can follow the yellow brick road to where you want to be, or you can remain stymied by that big wall that seals off any progress you want to make. It all depends on how you look at the obstacles. . . .

The point is that perspective is all about how we choose to see things. Because we look as much with our mind as with our eyes, we tend to "see" what we expect to see or want to see. Changing our perspective calls for a willingness to see things differently. That's the key to developing a positive attitude regardless of what happens to us.

Barbara Johnson
*Mama, Get the Hammer!*

# PROMISES ABOUT CHASING AWAY PRIDE

By pride comes nothing but strife,
But with the well-advised is wisdom.

🖾 Proverbs 13:10

The poor shall eat and be satisfied;
Those who seek Him will praise the LORD.
Let your heart live forever!

🖾 Psalm 22:26

Do not overwork to be rich;
Because of your own understanding, cease!
Will you set your eyes on that which is not?
For riches certainly make themselves wings;
They fly away like an eagle toward heaven.

🖾 Proverbs 23:4–5

LORD, my heart is not haughty,
Nor my eyes lofty.
Neither do I concern myself with great matters,
Nor with things too profound for me.

🖾 Psalm 131:1

# CHASING AWAY PRIDE

o you think anything concerning you right now is too small?

Your house or apartment? Your personal reputation? Your influence? Your job?

Your family (you want to add a spouse or children)? Your circle of friends? Your salary? Your life?

Until I paid attention to Psalm 131 I chafed. Then I discovered that God's leash wasn't too tight—my heart was too proud! I thought I "deserved" more; my self-image had greater expectations, and that attitude was the very grease on which I slid into self-pity, discontent, ungratefulness, misery.

Then I fixed my eyes on Jesus—and in my own eyes I became smaller and smaller. What was my stature, my purity, my power, my excellence compared with His? I felt foolish, embarrassed, very small.

Anne Ortlund
*Fix Your Eyes on Jesus*

# PROMISES ABOUT
# DELIGHTING IN GOD

Show me Your ways, O LORD;
Teach me Your paths.
Lead me in Your truth and teach me.
For You are the God of my salvation;
On You I wait all the day.

Psalm 25:4–5

Then you shall delight yourself in the LORD;
And I will cause you to ride on the high hills
    of the earth,
And feed you with the heritage of Jacob
    your father.
The mouth of the LORD has spoken.

Isaiah 58:14

*Every day I will bless You,*
*And I will praise Your name forever*
*and ever.*

Psalm 145:2

# DELIGHTING IN GOD

hat would you ask for if God offered you anything you desired? Would you ask for long life or riches or protection for those you love? Would you ask for wisdom or a deeper relationship with Him? When your wakeful mind isn't alert to tell you what you should ask for, would your unconscious heart ask for something that would please God?

Psalm 37, a psalm of David, tells us that if we delight ourselves in the Lord, He will give us the desires of our heart. Some people have said that this means that if we are seeking the Lord first, our desires will conform to His. I like to think that it actually means that God places the desires there to begin with.

Mary Hampton
*Tea and Inspiration*

# ACKNOWLEDGMENTS

*Grateful acknowledgment is made to the following publishers and copyright holders for permission to reprint copyrighted material:*

Kathy Babbitt, *Habits of the Heart* (Brentwood, Tenn.: Wolgemuth & Hyatt, 1990).

Jan Carlberg, *The Hungry Heart* (Brentwood, Tenn.: Wolgemuth & Hyatt 1991).

Claire Cloninger, *When God Shines Through* (Dallas: Word, 1988, 1994).

Verdell Davis, *Riches Stored in Secret Places* (Dallas:Word, 1994).

Elisabeth Elliot, *The Shaping of a Christian Family* (Nashville: Thomas Nelson, 1992).

Gloria Gaither, *Decisions* (Alexandria: Gaither Family Resources, 1996) 800/955-8746 Gaither Family Resources, P.O. Box 737, Alexandria, IN 46001.

Mary Hampton, *Tea and Inspiration* (Nashville: Thomas Nelson 1995).

Liz Curtis Higgs, *Only Angels Can Wing It: The Rest of Us Have to Practice* (Nashville: Thomas Nelson, 1995).

Barbara Jenkins, *Wit and Wisdom for Women* (Nashville: Thomas Nelson, 1996)

Barbara Johnson, *I'm So Glad You Told Me What I Didn't Wanna Hear* (Dallas: Word, 1996).

——*Mama, Get the Hammer! There's a Fly on Papa's Head* (Dallas: Word, 1994).

——*Stick a Geranium in Your Hat and Be Happy* (Dallas: Word, 1990).

Laura Lewis Lanier, *All Things Bright and Beautiful* (Norwalk, Conn.: C. R. Gibson, 1995).

Gail MacDonald, *High Call, High Privilege* (Wheaton, Ill.: Tyndale, 1984).

Anne Ortlund, *Fix Your Eyes on Jesus* (Dallas: Word, 1991).

——*Disciplines of the Heart* (Dallas: Word, 1987).

Edith Schaeffer, *The Tapestry* (Dallas: Word, 1981).

Elizabeth Skoglund, *Safety Zones: Finding Refuge in Times of Turmoil* (Dallas: Word, 1986).

Luci Swindoll, *You Bring the Confetti* (Dallas: Word, 1986, 1997).

Joni Eareckson Tada, *Seeking God* (Brentwood, Tenn.: Wolgemuth and Hyatt, 1991).

Mary Whelchel, *How to Thrive from 9 to 5* (Dallas: Word, 1995).

Susan Alexander Yates, *A House Full of Friends* (Colorado Springs: Focus on the Family, 1995) © Susan Alexander Yates.